THE
Who
THAT IS YOU

Who, What, When, Where Why = WORTH

SHANNON MAGEE

BALBOA.PRESS

A DIVISION OF HAY HOUSE

Balboa Press books may be ordered through booksellers or by contacting:

Balboa Press
A Division of Hay House
1663 Liberty Drive
Bloomington, IN 47403
www.balboapress.com
844-682-1282

Print information available on the last page.

ISBN: 978-1-9822-6201-3 (sc)
ISBN: 978-1-9822-6202-0 (e)

Balboa Press rev. date: 01/20/2021

It only takes one moment to remember the truth of who you are. Within the simplicity of your breath, you can find experiences and inspiration!

In one simple inhale, you can soften your body and create space in your heart. The judgmental voices in your mind can become distant, and you can recall that life is a gift. When you learn to appreciate and use the bounty of your breath, you awaken to what you have arrived to do!

As many times I have allowed fear to be my fuel, I have also caught myself in moments of grace, reminding me to remain present and walk openly into the consciousness of life.

It is my highest Intention that you find yourself in grace, that you unlock the chains of the past to reveal the truth of your purpose.

We are sentient beings, given this consciousness to acquire grace through observation, forgiveness, and Gratitude. As such, we are on this planet to transform and transcend the barriers of the ego. We have opportunities to be of service to our fellow man to fulfill our life's purpose!

As you begin this journey with me, I only ask for one thing, trust. Trust in the process. Rebirthing into your worth is not easy; it will force you to become uncomfortable. However, if you have gotten this far on your path to transformation, your heart innately seeks the truth. Your soul seeks the space to shine!

You are worthy of abundance in all areas of your life, my friends. There has been wrongdoing, illness, abuse, and trauma that has no authority over your ability to live an abundant and joyful life! You were born for this gift!

Life has offered you many choices and directions. It is innate to seek and desire change. Finding the path that reveals your purpose will award you the experiences you deserve, your birthright! Welcome to the journey!

This book is inspired to guide you through reflection and movement gently and with compassion. I offer my shoulder to lean on, my hand to hold, and my wisdom as your tool.

Each chapter is an experience in aligning your energetic body to teach you how to create new directions of thought. You will recognize a consistency within the content and hopefully use your inner guidance for diving deep within the practices.

Who, what, when, where, why equals worth! It's time to discover!

I was in a deep sleep when awakened with a racing heart! All the changes that I had made in my life led me to the moment when my higher-self forcefully moved me to pay attention.

For years my students, family, my community had been dropping subtle hints that I had more to share from a larger platform than how I was already living and working. I repeatedly dismissed the gentle nudging from the universe. For me, it just wasn't the right time.

How little did I realize that I had manifested the right time through my constant fear-based thoughts? All arrows pointed to the moment as I sat writing this to you. Without a doubt, I am willing and confident to share my stories, lessons, and guidance. Through these processes, you will hit the rewind button in your mind to identify the events, thoughts, and actions that have kept you unhappy, unfulfilled, and continuously seeking your purpose. Through practice, you can create, come into alignment with your true self, transform, and give thanks. You will rejoice when you have finally arrived in your worth, wholly enveloped in grace!

My higher self, which, in my perception, is God's consciousness, the voice of the Divine speaking directly to me, believes that with this practice, you will arrive within yourself transformed and healthy!

Now, I am not a Doctor; I do not hold any degrees that carry weight or authority, nor can I diagnose any emotional or behavioral conditions. These practices are not a prescription to heal you; they are a means to transform your life. What I am is a vessel of information. I am a combination of my life lessons, training, and experiences with intuitive gifts. I hear, trust, and believe in my inspired thought!

Throughout my life, I have, like you, endured pain. When I was a child, I was a victim of sexual abuse and a product of divorce. As a teenager, I was a victim of bullying. As a young adult, I was lost and acting out. As a woman, I was emotionally abused, shredded of any remnants of self-worth that I may have had. I survived to lose my home to a tragedy, all personal possessions, and a life change that left me broken. I was physically sick from PTSD, alone, and a single mother to three small children with little to start over.

But start over, I did, and in as little as 18 months, with very little, built a thriving business based on community, peace, and wellness. Five years later, I expanded my business. I have taught thousands of hours of self-empowerment through classes and workshops. I have led international retreats, speaking engagements and successfully navigated my journey of discovering my self-worth.

But things have changed. I like us all got caught in my fear. I was too busy to listen to the gentle whispers of Spirit, encouraging me to look within. When we choose to ignore the small signs that we are not working in alignment with our purpose, we will inevitably create experiences that will force us to halt and hopefully change. After nearly losing my life to a pulmonary embolism, I chose to abandon the only definition of myself that I have grown to depend on to be here with you. I hope you will begin to trust me, your path, and your transformation through this decision.

Everything you want to know about your life lives on the other side of the wall of fear you have manifested. When you do not question your circumstances, you build a strong barrier of limitations, blocking your understanding of your purpose. You may perceive your life as a collection of thoughts, feelings, and emotions that create experiences that you interpret as safe. Despite experiencing chaos and pain, you have surrendered to remain in this reality. Your manifested experiences allow you to predict your future without even thinking about it! Your repetitive thoughts have become a habit, creating similar low vibrational feelings. These feelings enable your mind and body to exist on autopilot.

To begin the process of transformation, you must observe your thoughts and create new routes of thinking. Modern science teaches us that through observation and meditation practice, we have the power to rewire the neuropathways in our minds for newly inspired ways of thinking. As I am actively observing, I have become excited about the changes I can see manifesting in my life. The law of attraction has finally become demystified! The loopholes in the Law of Attraction that I once accepted as knowledge far beyond my comprehension is no longer cosmic faith. There is now concrete evidence that change can and will happen if there is a dedicated practice of meditation and discipline of thought!

Throughout our lives, we have heard the multitude of stories of people who have survived and healed the most devastating diagnoses. You may personally know people who have overcome high odds. So what is it that sets these individuals aside from the rest of humanity? You are a creation just the same as these self-healing humans. You similarly have one heart that beats, two lungs that breathe, systems in your body that work just like everyone else's. There is one defining difference you think; differently, that is all. Simple enough to remedy, do you agree?

Your body and mind are miraculous! You are a transformation machine! Your body and mind work 24 hours a day, seven days a week, to accomplish one task—your body and mind work to create homeostasis (balance). Your body has an innate ability to do this, given a supported environment, working diligently to produce balance every day. Your body, however, follows the chemicals produced by your emotions. This autonomic response creates an imbalance. In a nutshell, by changing your thoughts, you change your life! Easier said than done, I know! Don't worry; I am here to help you!

Let's talk a little bit about innate knowledge. It is not as foreign as you think, it is you, and you are one within it. This knowledge within your being is intrinsic— directed by the flow of energy generated by what you think and feel.

The environment in which it moves through is how your innate operates. Here is a simple definition of how it works.

Let's say you have a broken bone. You do exactly what your history has directed you to do. Through life, you have witnessed healing on the outside of your body. You do not question this healing because you had seen your body healing you before your very eyes since you were a child. You know it will happen!

You go to the doctor who performs an exam and determines if a cast is needed to repair the break. But, is it the cast that is healing the injury? No, it is not. The cast is merely creating an environment for the body's innate to go into action and do its job!

You do not question this process, and you do not doubt it is happening; you simply follow the instructions and wait for it to heal, not giving it a second thought! Things change, though, when you can no longer see the injury. Have you ever noticed how fear-based you become when the wounds are on the inside? When you can't see your physical or emotional injuries, fear takes over! When you can not see the healing happening, you spiral into worry?

When the body becomes imbalanced through chemicals produced from fearful habitual thinking and feeling, it will manifest itself through dis-ease! The same wisdom that heals us on the outside heals us on the inside. The one roadblock in this process is how you think about the healing. You typically doubt it is happening; you are fearful; you do not trust your body. This habitual thinking produces low vibrational thoughts. This low vibration then creates emotions that support an environment within the body that is not conducive to healing.

My goal is to arm you with the tools to create an environment within your mind and body to aid you in your life progression. Reaching your goals, be it supreme health and well being, financial success, fulfilling relationships, mended emotional wounds, are all attainable when the proper environment creates within your thoughts.

I have created a process for you as a beginner to discover transformation within this book. Through my own life experiences, the traumas that I have personally worked to overcome through years of spiritual study, and my expertise as an energy practitioner, guide, and teacher have led me to acquire a toolbox of information to help support and guide your process. This method is five simple steps to living with more quality to your life. When I ask my students what it is they want, the answer is always the same. "I only want to be happy." Happiness is the foundation for all desires in life. If happiness is what you seek, then let's begin!

Week One: Who

I am sure you have asked yourself these questions thousands of times in your life!

Who am I, or who am I supposed to be? The answer is left in the ethers as we are continually trying to discover this very definition of self! This search becomes complicated, for as you grow, you evolve. Through your life experiences, you become the manifestation of your beliefs, but your limitations are even more significant.

I firmly believe that to achieve your goals, you must begin where you want to land! Your intuition compass will continue to pull you in many different directions until you have a clear understanding of your endpoint. Let's begin by answering some questions. All the questions in this book are designed to help you reflect upon your life choices and to observe where you currently reside within yourself and where you want to be.

- **How have you been defining yourself?**

- **What is the story that your mind tells you day in and day out about your life experiences?**

- **What are you thinking and feeling about your current life circumstances?**

- **Do you remain in a place of seeking, or do you take action and move towards creating?**

Take some time now to reflect upon your answers. For the sake of this journey and what you will discover, I ask that you designate a journal or notebook specifically for this experience. You will find the information you retrieve from yourself will be a reference point that you can return to throughout your life challenges.

Through this journey, you will discover the answers you seek to define your purpose and compassionately transform your life.! Take a few moments to journal some reflections on these questions.

- **Do the choices you make daily come from self-love or unworthiness?**

- **How do you define self-love?**

- **If you were living a life of self-love, how would that life appear to you?**

Dive deep here. You have given your entire life to endeavors that have not served your purpose; now is the time to commit to these changes. You may find that digging deep will invoke uncomfortable emotions. It is ok! Nobody sees these answers, but you. Be raw; tell the truth no matter how much it makes your stomach ache, no matter how hard it is. Remember, the one promise I made to you, this would not be easy. Be descriptive. You are doing this work because you have a higher goal! Do not be afraid! These questions beckon you to observe your current ways of thinking and then transform your thoughts to create abundance and prosperity; you may find it difficult, depending on how much you genuinely love yourself. For me, in the beginning, I struggled with going big with my desires. I discovered that I did not believe I deserved the life of my dreams!

Let's continue:

- **How would it feel to love yourself completely?**

- **If you could paint the canvas of your life based on self-love, what would you see?**

- **Where would you be living?**

- **What type of career would you have chosen?**

- **Who are the people that influence you, and where are they within your sphere?**

- **What kind of lifestyle would you have if there were no financial limitations?**

Take as much time as you need to describe these answers. Describe in color and depth! Be detailed; they will, in the end, be your landing point! In your responses, you will discover your goals!

This part of the journey can be frustrating. None of us have arrived within ourselves today without experiencing a wealth of pain. We have moved through life for most of us, thinking we were making the best possible choices. I reassure you that you have. You did nothing wrong, and you did not fail. All of your experiences have been lessons that have brought you to the now. It is now that your changes are happening.

Now that you have pondered your answers and have described the life you desire to your best knowledge, please take those answers deeper. Take them to an even higher vibration! Take some time to look at each answer and ask yourself, is this as far as I can reach, or can I go further now? Keep writing, do not be afraid to embrace what your higher self reveals to you!

The mind, your thoughts, your feelings, and their contribution to your life experiences.

From your inception, in your Mother's womb, your mind began to wire itself for thought. Since all thought is energy, even the thoughts of your Mother became part of your hardwiring. Everything your Mother experienced had an energetic vibration that left an imprint within you! Through science, thoughts and feelings are measured and given a frequency. Similar to a radio wave, so is what you think and feel. All matter is this way. All things in our existence and beyond have a vibration.

Now begins the journey of creating more neuropathways of thought. Everything you have ever seen, touched, tasted, smelled, experienced creates your programming. From age zero to 5-6 years old, you make the blueprint of your life experience. This blueprint is the lens through which you subconsciously view your life. Sorry to say this is the pitfall. Comprised in this blueprint is fear, born from pain. There are only two emotions for our foundation that support us, fear and love. For most, fear overrides all other feelings. Fear feeds worry, anger, resentment, bitterness, frustration, and pain. These powerful emotions have become your program.

Now, of course, life is not all misery! There is joy, happiness, peace, and pleasure. To no fault of your own, fear dominates who you have become. Historically fear is where most of your thoughts reside. You might very well be trying hard to eliminate the dominating emotions of fear. However, the chemicals produced by it becomes what the mind seeks, therefore inevitably addicted to these thoughts. The result is more fear, which leads to stagnation, lack of motivation, in some loss and dis-ease.

Do not dismay my friends; hope is not lost! There is a way to reverse the program!

A personal story:

As a child, an abusive home was not my environment. I, however, did have experiences that were violating and full of shame. There were incidences of sexual abuse, bullying, and emotional abandonment. All of these very tragic and toxic wrongdoings created an indelible mark on who I would eventually become.

As a young adult, my decisions were based purely on emotion. I was impulsive and needed immediate gratification. I was incapable of taking time to think things through. What was directly in front of me was the only option I saw. Never did I take the time to discern what was most healthy or productive logically. I was reactive. This behavior often leads to potentially dangerous situations: excessive drinking, promiscuous sex, loss of self. For me, it was my reality. If the path meant hard work, I did not want to take it. The need to be gratified outweighed the commitment to discipline for long term rewards. Marrying this behavior with the fight or flight response that was my coping mechanism inevitably to flee any uncomfortable situation created a program of action that sent me into a downward spiral. I will share with you later the incredible impact all of this had on my adult life and how I ended up spending 14 years in a very toxic relationship, unhappy and alone. What was formed from the experiences of my childhood was a program of fear and diminished self-worth. Circumstances beyond my control created the pathway to a lifetime of struggle. The condition of thoughts in my subconscious was the lens through which I viewed my life, without my awareness.

Due to my impulsive nature, my mind and body became dependent on the emotions reactive thinking produced. I had become merely the container that held my repetitive thoughts. I was not aware, awake, or alive. I was only existing. I lived this way, in and out of consciousness, for most of my adult life. Though deeply rooted in the existential experience, always seeking growth and enlightenment, I could not, no matter how hard I worked on it, shed my programming to make healthy choices. I would have times of growth and healing, yet it took the complete disassembling of my life as I knew it to catapult my awareness into something more significant than it had ever experienced to be. Not until I implemented observation and a dedication to disciplined practices in Yoga and meditation did I finally see how I was relating to the world around me.

As children, we develop self-worth through love and compassion. Our environments should provide safety and security. When these essential needs are absent, the well of love that should sustain us as adults does not exist, creating a thinking pattern that inevitably dictates our actions. Through observation and taking action through practice, these synapses rewire to fire new thought, manifesting feelings that are the opposite of our habitual experiences. We must do things differently. We must lift the needle from the record that has been playing the song of our lives. The time is now to record your song of success and happiness!

Mission Statement:

In life, you can not know where you are going until you embrace where you currently reside within yourself with a new lens. You must assume where you are from your highest vibration, from a place of abundance, strength, and love! With each step in the journey, you must define with positivity your foundation.

Just like an entrepreneur, to begin any business endeavor, one must develop a mission statement that clearly defines the wholeness of the product they wish to sell. You are your product! You are selling yourself to yourself! Understanding who you desire to be is empowering, mainly because you already are this person! Your body and mind already recognize this energy as your truth. With each step in this journey, make your statement to determine the final value of your worth! As you move through this healing process, following these steps, you will effortlessly arrive as you observe the unraveling of fear to reveal the Who that is You!

Your mission statement is your landing point. Your mission statement defines how you want the world to treat you. Your mission statement teaches the world through your boundaries how you value yourself!

My mission statement is a continuum of my evolution. As I grow and heighten my energetic frequencies, I expect more from myself. My mission statement is a continuous marker of my goals and perceptions. Here is an example of one of the first mission statements I wrote to define my "who."

"I, Shannon, with all that I am, live the values of integrity, love, loyalty, and compassion. I will live each day in the energy of my values. I will model my values through my words and actions. From my values, I will manifest my vibrational path of success and abundance! My way will be that of light and

love from the foundation that living in my values creates. My values define who I am!"

Take some time now to create your mission statement to define your "**Who**." Dig deep! Remember that we teach people how to treat us by how much we value ourselves. Be it through business or personal relationships; people will treat you through what you will allow. Boundaries are always appropriate when they derive from compassion for yourself and others.

To create your mission statement, first, ask yourself these questions.

- **What values morally define me?**

- **What has happened in my past that has not aligned with my values?**

- **What emotions have I felt from not being in alignment with my values?**

- **If I could use one word to describe my values, what would it be?**

When I began this book, it was my sole Intention to take all of my wisdom, best practices, and healing to turn these elements into a useful tool for you to use. I wanted to help you create a toolbox of transformation to heal your life and manifest the best version of yourself. It has been exciting to observe my higher self dictate the path this process takes. This process is in constant evolution as I write. In real-time, this process evolves and morphs into something greater! I see my metamorphosis continue as I share it with you. I am observing how much I have to give! Again, this direction is coming straight from Spirit! I am happy to allow this guidance to channel through me this way.

The practice of Yoga and Meditation:

In my opinion, one of the simplest ways to evolve and manifest is through Yoga and meditation! I began my journey in Yoga and meditation in my early twenties. I have always had an interest in spiritual enlightenment, and from a young age, I found a salve for my wounds in Yoga.

As I touched on earlier, due to my need for instant gratification, Yoga was by far a practice that ignited me due to its fast results.

In my early years, I practiced Kundalini yoga more interested in the spiritual enlightenment results it offered than the physical practice. It was not until I turned forty, having survived a significant trauma of losing my home to a fire and my marriage of 14 years all in one week, did I embrace the physical practice as a means to heal.

I began the practice of Restorative Yoga and Vinyasa yoga as a way to escape. I found through the physical practice of Vinyasa yoga an emptiness of my mind. My body would generate heat through the training, burning off my thoughts of pain. I would come to my yoga mat to escape, as it was the only reprieve I could find that had such immediate results. Learning how to use my breath to expand and contract my body helped me heal and feel amazing. My mind became more positive! I knew with each inhale I was taking in life.

By setting intentions and marrying those intentions with my physical practice, I constructed the perfect environment in my mind for my transformation.

Eventually, I found myself in a Restorative yoga class. Restorative Yoga was a much different experience than what my Vinyasa practice offered. Restorative Yoga is an energetic healing modality of meditation and the gentle, supportive opening of the body through postures. It uses props to support the physical body so the nervous system can come to a place of rest. One hour of Restorative Yoga is equivalent to 3 hours of sleep on the nervous system! This practice, in the beginning, for me, was harrowing. The restorative Yoga method requires the practitioner to silence the mind and let go of the physical body, so there may be energy movement through the chakras. At the beginning of learning this practice, I would weep. I was unable to make it through one class without feeling anxious. The release of energy was so powerful. I could fully feel it coursing through me! Eventually, through discipline and repetitive practice, I learned to stay in the postures longer. Overtime I indeed receive the healing benefits of the training. This healing comes in reducing cortisol (your stress hormone), overall well-being, restful sleep, and a more positive outlook!

After seeing a therapist for a few months, PTSD was my diagnosis, which, over time, manifested in many physical and emotional symptoms. The year directly following the loss of my home and my divorce, I experienced daily panic attacks and anxiety. I had sensations of suffocation, elevated heart rate, and tachycardia; my reality felt like a living hell. I had lightheadedness, sleep deprivation, racing thoughts, and experienced pain in many areas of my body, especially the abdomen. I lost my short term memory, my face became numb, and I would convulse when I would try to rest. My breathing was always shallow, and I had repetitive night terrors that would force me to awaken, covered in sweat with my heart racing. With many emergency room visits and hospitalization due to a severe kidney infection, something had to give! The practice of Yoga slowly restored My health and gave me back a quality of life!

I fell in love with the practice of Vinyasa yoga and Restorative Yoga. It did not take long for me to witness and experience the life-changing results yoga was offering to my life. Over time my symptoms began to lessen. After a year, I was symptom-free.

After a few months of practice, I enrolled in a 200-hour teacher training for Vinyasa yoga and completed a 20-hour teacher training in Restorative Yoga. After three months of graduating from my training, I opened a yoga studio and co/ wrote a certification curriculum for Restorative Yoga. I truly wanted to create a space of healing through Yoga for my community! My journey was a testament to the incredible healing Yoga and Meditation offered.

Since then, I have taught thousands of hours in both Vinyasa and Restore. I have hosted hundreds of yoga, meditation, and energy healing workshops and co-lead international yoga retreats! I speak on the practice of Restorative Yoga to large organizations and train teachers on how to lead the practice!

I have studied Yoga's philosophy and daily discipline in meditation and Gratitude through my yoga practice years. I believe that developing training in both the physical practice of Yoga and mediation are the building blocks to success in anyone's life journey!

The physical practice of Yoga, in my opinion, is only 10% of your yoga practice! Yoga is transcendent! Yoga is, in my opinion, some kind of magic that surpasses the ego to allow the truth to reveal itself to the student! It is not necessary to be an advanced yogi to acquire the healing benefits yoga offers. The only requirement is to have the Intention to heal. Coming to your yoga mat consistently offers you a space to process your emotions.

Your emotions are signals to the mind to create more thoughts that will, in turn, ignite more feelings. Coming to your yoga mat and practicing Yoga does a few things for your body.

The practice of Yoga creates "Prana" this is life force energy, experienced as "Heat" in the body. When you marry an intention (a thought) with the physical practice, otherwise known as "Asana," you powerfully create change!

Your body fills with heat, and because your thoughts are energy, the prana burns off the unwanted energy and ignites the power of new thought (your Intention.)

Yoga is where the magic happens! Through the repetition of this practice, your overall health and mental state begin to repair. The process of change overrides all barriers and begins to articulate into your life! You start to become the most authentic version of yourself!

To develop your self-healing toolbox, you will put into action a series of yoga postures, also known as "Asana" I have chosen each position specifically for your healing in each area of the process. When you have completed the work, you will have a short but effective and accessible yoga practice to enhance your life each day!

In this chapter, you are working on discovering the Who, that is you! The posture you will practice now (with my direction) will give you a greater sense of who you are! This yoga posture opens your heart space through a four-part breathing technique to create the sensation of identity. As you consciously breathe into your heart, you not only expand within yourself, but you also hold space for your Intention. It is vital to be an observer in the early stages of your yoga practice. Keep your journal nearby so you can record your thoughts. Write down what you think and feel as you come out of your physical Asana and your meditation. You will find great healing generated through your record of ideas as you reflect upon their meaning.

Sukasana- Easy Seat:

Practicing Sukasana is easy. There is no wrong way to do Yoga ever! Simply allow yourself to be in the experience. Do not label or judge what you observe. Often, in the beginning stages of yoga practice, the mind is controlled by the ego. It is not uncommon to hear thoughts of worry or to feel frustrated; it is a normal part of the practice! As time goes on, I promise you will be delighted to one day notice the ego's elements are no longer present.

To begin Sukasana, find yourself seated comfortably on your yoga mat or the floor. In this pose, you will remain seated. If you do not have a yoga mat, I do encourage you to purchase one. Your yoga mat will become your valued space, your trusted holding place to which you retreat.

Sit with legs crossed, and notice your posture. If you are slumping over with rounded shoulders, bring length into your spine. Soften your jaw and release your tongue from the roof of your mouth. Notice your breath. Notice if your breath moves deeply into your belly or stops short shallow in your chest. Breathe with your normal breath here. Be an observer of your breath at the moment you are inhaling and exhaling. What do you feel within your body? Notice any areas of tension or discomfort. Perhaps ask your body why it feels this way. You will be surprised as you move through this process of how your body speaks to you. You will also begin to talk to your body in a much different way. You will notice how critical you are of your body, and you will adopt a language of love, gently encouraging your body to become healthy and showing its resilience and perseverance! Over time you will marvel at your body's ability to respond to your commands and encouragement!

Evenly root down to the earth by rearranging your sits' bones. Be in this space now for a few natural breaths.

Let's begin to create ***pranayama.*** Pranayama is the regulation of breath through a variety of techniques.

In this Asana, you will practice "Samavritti," which means equal movement. This breathwork is a four-part breathing sequence. This type of breath calms the body and helps remove the mind's distractions to enhance meditation.

The four parts to this practice consist of inhalation, hold, exhalation, and an expel.

Let's begin:

- *Inhale, two, three, four*
- *Hold, two, three, four*
- *Exhale, two, three, four*
- *Expel, two, three, four*

The goal of this practice is to cultivate an equal count of breath throughout the practice without strain. Continue practicing Samavritt. Notice how your heart space expands with your breath. Observe the sensations in your body. Acknowledge the emptiness in your mind. When practicing four-part breathing, your mind is absent of thought. If you are new to meditation, if emptying your mind is a challenge, use the practice of Samavritti.

Meditation:

The subconscious mind is a great vortex, deeply layered and complex. The theta brain receives inspiration and guidance from the higher self (otherwise known as the "Super Conscious Mind"). It is in the subconscious that thousands upon thousands of thoughts circulate every minute of your life.

The most significant thing about the subconscious mind, in my opinion, is how it ultimately experiences your thoughts as reality. The subconscious is similar to a toddler. What you tell it, it believes it to be so. Healing happens through thinking this way! There is no divide in the subconscious. What happens in your external world and what happens in your mind is the same!

What get's me excited is this, you don't have to spend thousands of dollars on an expensive vacation to some luxurious resort to receive the healing benefits of the experience. You need only to imagine the experience in your mind, and your body will respond as if you are truly living the experience externally. The more you practice engaging the subconscious through vivid journeys of self-healing and experiences of joy, the more your mind will begin to relate those experiences to feelings of joy and happiness, health, and well being. Inevitably over time, this will become your program! After time and practice, your subconscious mind will link these experiences to similar events in your external world that create the same feelings.

Soon you will have a snowball effect of thought; you will have created a habit of thinking from a place of positivity. Your body will then continue to produce emotions that align with your ideas. Change then occurs!

Guided meditation and visualization are the methods you will use to promote change and catapult you to your goals. As you take your mind through a vivid journey, your body will have an emotional response, which will create a memory in your account. These compelling emotions will act as a magnet to similar feelings you will experience in your conscious reality. You are drawing into your life experiences, which will create the same feelings.

If this all sounds super confusing, like a bunch of gobbly gooks, don't worry! You do not have to understand the semantics of it all to receive the benefits of the practice! By merely taking yourself through visualized meditation, you create an environment in your mind that produces emotions that will transform your mind and body. Your soul will smile at you!

This mediation comes directly from my Source of energy as I relate it to channeled from the Divine. I have meditated and asked for you to receive healing. Through the visualization that is being gifted to you here, I hope you will connect with your Source, your higher self, your subconscious mind, and all sentient beings that work on your behalf! This mediation is to give you the experience of who you are, void of ego. This mediation unmasks the low vibration of fear to allow the light that is you to shine brightly and for your body to experience this as love. All goodness comes from love. Love is the Source of all that is right, good, and real within you.

Take a moment to find a comfortable space where you will be uninterrupted for the next 15 minutes. You may lay down or remain seated for this meditation. Once you memorize this meditation, you will quickly take yourself through the visualization with ease. Remember, meditating with visualization is teaching your subconscious mind to experience emotions that vibrate at higher frequencies. Over time, you will rewire your neuropathways of thought as you continually direct new experiences to replace fear.

Begin by focusing on your breath, your slow natural inhalation, and exhalation. Soften your jaw, release your tongue from the roof of your mouth, and soften your face's muscles. Be sure to have your body supported through this meditation. Your mind will become distracted if your body is uncomfortable.

Slow inhale, slow, deep exhale. As you breathe, constrict the muscles of the back of your throat. This way, tightening your muscles will create a sound like the ocean, allowing you to go deeper into your breath.

Feel the weight of your eyelids over your eyes. Feel your eyelids heavy and relaxed. With your next inhalation, bring your awareness into the souls of your feet. Feel your feet heavy and at ease. Breathe in and draw your attention to your legs. Feel the weight of your legs right where you are. Encourage your legs to become heavy and relaxed with your exhalation. Feel your hips; draw your breath deeply into your hips. Experience your hips softening with each deep inhale and exhale.

Deep breath in, feel your belly expand as your breath fills your torso. Experience each rib separate creating space for your inspiration to open your heart. Your collar bone expands and broadens.

Now direct your mind to the palms of your hands. Feel energy swarming around and around in the palms of your hands. Feel this energy move into your arms and up to your shoulders as you inhale.

Long deep inhale, long deep exhale.

With your next inhalation, bring your awareness to the space between your eyebrows, your third eye. Long deep inhale, long deep exhale. Feel the weight of your eyelids, and you bring your consciousness into this deep space within your mind. Feel the area all around you. Feel the space as energy. Space is above you, below you, on either side of you, in front of you, and behind you. With every breath you take in, this space expands even greater.

Now, with your eyes remaining closed, peer deeply into the space between your eyebrows. See before you a long dark tunnel. See this as if you were watching a movie in your mind. In the distance, you see a sphere of golden light. This sphere slowly spins. You experience this sphere of light as knowledge.

Take a deep inhale into your heart space. As you breathe in, you draw this sphere of knowledge in the form of light closer to you. With every inhale, the light becomes brighter, but it is not blinding; you see it. It is gentle. Finally, this sphere of knowledge is right before you. Reach out your hand, as this light intuitively knows to rest in your palm.

Long deep inhale, long deep exhale. Place this sphere of light against your abdomen. Experience the warmth of this knowledge as it enters into your physical body. This sphere of light intuitively knows where to go. This energetic healing energy is a salve to all areas within you that seek healing, emotionally or physically.

Experience this light with your breath. With every inhale, this light expands, reaching out beyond the limits of your ego as this light's energy forces the layers of fear to fall away to reveal to you your true self. Your highest vibration!

Be in this experience. Allow your mind to accept this wholeheartedly. As you stay vibrating with your breath, repeat this affirmation in your mind.

"I am the manifestation of love."

Come back to the awareness of your breath. With each inhales, repeat, "I am the manifestation of love" As you say, these words feel the inner workings of your mind, responding to this command's vibrational frequencies. "I am the manifestation of Love."

Slowly begin to bring your awareness to your physical body. Feel your body as you sit in your space. Feel the weight of your body. Notice how a sense of ease and peace cultivates through your meditation. Trust your work is complete.

When you are ready to locate your journal, it is time to give thanks!

Practice of Gratitude:

Part of your healing process is giving thanks. Gratitude is the simplest way to feel better. The act of appreciation creates healing energy, as well as cultivates future forward-thinking. Gratitude holds a high vibration, and it will bring you to your landing point, make an overall sense of well being, and adds a touch of closure to any healing practice.

For this practice of Gratitude, please take some time to reflect on the experience of your meditation.

Title your gratitude practice with "I am grateful for healing through meditation because it has taught me..."

Write at least one paragraph. Listen to what your higher self is bringing to light for you through this journaling exercise.

For the first week, you will repeat the practice outlined for you. I encourage you to carve out one hour a day for your transformation. Begin with rereading and repeating your mission statement aloud, moving through your short yoga practice, followed by meditation, journaling, and Gratitude. Go back and revisit the answers to your questions. As you dig deeper into your subconscious mind and release your limitations, your thoughts will expand to a higher level of awareness. Practice Gratitude each day by writing the answer to what your meditation practice has taught you. Take time to feel your emotions. Observe what is released and fully be in the experience of your feelings—Journal your revelations.

You have just gone through the practice of connecting with your higher self. Your higher self is all-knowing. Your higher self is your direct connection to your Divine

Source of energy. I hope that you will come to know your higher self as your most trusted companion, your guide, and caretaker in time.

I have been told in my life that we do not base life decisions on our intuition. I have been told this in my personal life as well as my professional life. I do not believe this to be the truth for me, nor do I accept it as truth. All of my major life decisions throughout my journey have come directly from the Divine.

Source speaks to my higher-self, my superconscious mind. I have worked for many years, heightening my vibration to connect with this energy. Now, in my life, I do not question inspired thought. I feel blessed to be in the realization of my truth. I trust and have faith in what I see, think, hear, and feel. It is through many life experiences that I have come to know myself this way. As you gradually make your way to defining your worth as love (you being that of love, only love, operating as love), you will learn to believe in yourself this way! What a spectacular way to live. Once you have complete trust in Source moving through life with this counsel is not without struggle but allows your life journey to navigate through a clear lens.

Week Two: WHAT

From childhood innocence, there have been significant life events that have determined how you view yourself as a human being. There have been events that have caused you to create specific perspectives. This perspective has become the reality to which you relate to the world around you. For many, "what is my life's purpose?" presents itself throughout life repeatedly. As you experience growth and change, your purpose takes different directions. Change is constant, and it is the most dependable factor in life; whether you like it or not.

Change does not come peacefully; it is not a gentle breeze blowing over you. Change in it's most potent form comes from pain and becoming incredibly uncomfortable. Transformation is the fierce storm that knocks you over and forces you to question everything you have ever told yourself about life as you know it to be.

Have you noticed that your story, the constant dialogue in your mind remains unchanged? Your account may have different characters, and perhaps the scene is different with each scenario. However, the underlying energy usually is the same, which brings us back to your program's original thoughts. Without changing the way you think about your life, if you do not do the work to rewire your thought pathways, you will inevitably continue to live out your story manifesting the same consequences in different experiences. Let's begin by defining these few questions. Use your journal to answer the items listed.

- **What has happened in your life that has provoked the desire for change?**

- **What was your original goal for your life? How has that goal changed through different experiences, and why?**

- **What inspires you? What ignites your heart space and makes you feel excited and motivated?**

- **What events in your life define your program? What trauma, crisis, or wrongdoing created your idea that you are not worthy of all you desire?**

- **What and who do you depend on in your life? How do these people or things show up for you?**

- **What brings you joy? What do you do for yourself that fills your cup?**

- **What causes you pain? Pain lives in the past; when we experience pain in our daily lives, our past wounds are still open.**

- **What do you do to enhance the lives of your family, friends, and strangers?**

As you work digging into your "**what's**," you will begin to notice more of **"who"** you are as a person living your life today.

Now, let's go back to the very first question, what has brought you to this state of wanting change? We don't just wake up one day and say, "Hey, I want to change my life; things are not working." For most of us, we are in a hamster wheel of discord. It amazes me how much we dismiss and how long we are willing to bear the weight of abuse, neglect, dis-ease, trauma, and unhappiness. There is always that one thing, the straw, so to speak, that is your endpoint. This one thing most likely manifests in a big way. We all have our aha moments when we have finally hit the wall of enough!

A personal story:

As I reflect upon my life, I can now easily see where I lost myself. I allowed other people to determine my future. My self-empowerment did not make my decisions, but fear of losing the relationships I was in decided for me. Based on fear, Ego kept me living isolated from freedom, a freedom to express myself, set goals, and accomplish them, freedom to choose for myself what was best. I completely surrendered to allowing others to decide what was best for me instead of following my hopes and dreams. When I was a young woman, I became separated from my identity; I lived my life as a shadow. I was not whole; my cup of self-worth was empty. I believed that someone else's success would be enough that my dreams were not worthy of fulfillment. I took to find fulfillment by surrendering my life to my relationships, good and bad. It took me years of pain to learn that changing your perception of how you relate to the world is the only answer. What becomes of your reality from there is the consequence of that change.

Mission Statement:

What you think about your life will be what fuels you and inevitably creates the experience you exist. It is essential to define your **"What"** and declare it to yourself as you vibrationally send it out into the world. Let's take a moment to ponder your definition of what you think you are?

You are a thinking, feeling human being. You have emotions that are important to you. The simple fact that you have chosen to read this book identifies this. Take a moment to bring your attention to what you tell yourself every day that defines what your life is. You can uncover this by just owning the repetitive thoughts that dominate your mind. Take a few moments to jot down what is present for you here.

In the past, my mind talk was very toxic. Over and over, I would tell myself that living unloved and unfulfilled was just the life I would have to live. I would replay the same dialogue of the victim. The thoughts were overwhelming, and as much as I tried distracting myself, my fearful thoughts were the never-ending theme of my life. I did not have a strategy to lift myself out of the gutter of despair and own my worth in those days. Hell, I would not even have been able to define what self-worth was back then. Had I had any self-love, I would not have remained living that way for as long as I did. The truth is, I was terrified. Fear dominated my thoughts daily. How would I care for my children, feed them, provide a good life for them? In my mind, I was willing to sacrifice my happiness for my children's stability until the time came when I could no longer deny my truth. I am worthy of love; I am worthy of respect and deserving of loyalty and compassion.

Creating a mission statement for what you are is essential. You declare your worth not only to yourself but to the world around you vibrationally! Remember how your body works? Your thoughts hold vibrational frequencies; every single cell in your body will energetically respond to your high vibration of self-worth!

I, _____ am light. I am dedicated, compassionate, love. I am the manifestation of all that is good, healthy, and loving. What I am is a beating heart that emanates from the world around me. What I am affects others through my goodness. What I am is peace within.

Take a few moments now to journal your Mission Statment of What you are to yourself. Allow the pen to flow freely with the thoughts that arise. Do not label or judge your thoughts; just allow them to be what they are. You may surprise yourself with what comes to mind!

Asana:

The practice of Yoga transcends all barriers. What we experience physically has a magical effect on our emotional bodies. The word Yoga means to "yolk," bringing together two things. Typically we bring together breath and movement. One of my favorite yoga postures is Tadasana, otherwise known as "Mountain Pose" I love this posture for the sturdiness it invokes within my physical body, for the strength I feel when I practice it. For the surge of energy, I experience drawing up from the center of the earth. As I relate this posture to "**What**" I want to be as I define my life, I revel in the notion of being like a mountain and all that entails. Strength, power, beauty! Often when people take a pilgrimage, they climb a mountain to conquer their fears and reach their goals. They learn lessons along the way and arrive at the summit victorious!

The practice of Tadasana may look simple. As you observe someone in this posture, it seems as if they are only just standing still. However, there is much more going on inside the body that requires concentration and discipline to remain. As I said, for the sake of this yoga practice, we will bring together the energy of two things thought and Asana. Combining this will ignite a flow of energy so powerful that the thought's vibration will become magnified into the universe! For this practice, create an affirmation in the form of "I am," for example, "I am powerful, I am loving, I am worthy." Take a few moments before you begin your practice to think about what you would like your affirmation to be. Use this affirmation every time you practice Tadasana and observe how the mind stays within the statement's content.

The practice of Tadasana: Mountain Pose

You do not need a yoga mat for this posture. However, I feel your yoga mat creates a unique and designated space for you to use for your healing. Be it on your mat, on the grass, a beach, or your living room floor; there is no denying the experience of Tadasana's strength and power!

Stand with your feet hip's width distance apart. With your eyes closed, bring your concentration to the souls of your feet. Take a deep breath in through your nose as you slowly become aware of the vibration of the earth beneath you.

Tap into your breath. Take a long, deep inhale, experiencing the coolness of your inhalation as it enters in through your nostrils. Feel your belly fill. Imagine a balloon filling with air. Your abdomen expands, and the breath fills you. As you exhale, consciously draw your navel towards your spine in a contraction, deflating your balloon. Your breath will rise into your chest, travel to your throat, and leave your body warm. Experience the sensation of the change in your breath as it leaves your body changed.

Bring your awareness back to the souls of your feet. Feel the vibration anchoring you firmly to the ground. Continue to breathe with appreciation as you take your next breath to draw the energy from the earth into your calves. Feel this energy, be in the experience of transforming into the mighty mountain that is you!

Contract your calves' muscles, and with your next inhalation, draw the earth's energy into your quadriceps. Lift your quadriceps off of your knees in a contraction. Roll the inner thighs towards one another; stay with your breath! (If you are having trouble engaging this way, the use of a yoga block between your inner thighs will help you) Place the block lengthwise between your legs and squeeze the block tightly. You will feel the engagement of your quadriceps while doing this. Over time you will be able to engage without the use of the prop.

Draw the energy now into your pelvis. Tuck your tailbone, and neutralize your pelvic floor and hips. Long deep inhale, long deep exhale.

Elongate your spine, pulling the energy through your upper body. Broaden your collar bone and drop your shoulders into their sockets. Imagine you have a string from the top of your head pulling you upward, as the energy of the earth anchors you firmly to the ground.

Stay engaged, stay contracted, stay aware! Remain in this posture for 5-10 long deep even breaths. Once complete, slowly shake out your body. Take a few moments to reflect on how your body feels.

Meditation:

Meditating on the **"What"** you can be not only very healing but also exciting! Your soul is continuously speaking to you. Your higher self is all-seeing and knowing and knows **WHAT** vibrational frequency you are. Meditating on your **"What"** helps release old wounds' while heightening your vibrational field of awareness and wholeness. Do this meditation every day in this week of **"What"** in conjunction with your yoga practice. Remember to journal any thoughts, images, and feelings you experience during the meditation. All of the information is provided by your higher self and is part of your healing process.

For this meditation, find a comfortable place to sit that is supportive for your back and neck. Be sure to dress comfortably. If your body temperature usually drops during meditation practice, have a blanket on top of you. It is essential not to be distracted by the body, telling you it's uncomfortable or too warm or chilly. If you are not a seasoned meditation practitioner, you will quickly become interrupted by your environment. Try to practice when you are not tired and alone without interruption for at least 15 minutes.

To bring yourself into awareness, I will ask that you get into your mind an intention for this meditation based on the work centered around your **"What."** This Intention does not have to be detailed but must hold an energy of purpose. State it aloud.

Shannon's Intention: I intend to receive healing through the practice of this meditation. I observe all images that my subconscious mind releases and my higher self reveals to me without judgment.

When you are ready, take a few deep cleansing breaths in and out through your nose—deeply inhaling and slowly exhaling. Feel your breath enter your body as your lungs expand. Direct your breath to the base of your spine, and as you exhale, contract your abdomen to release your breath back into the atmosphere entirely. Continue this five times or until you feel relaxed and your mind is empty.

If your mind remains full of chatter and distraction, continue deep breathing until you are ready.

Feel your body in its container. Feel your body fully as if you are experiencing your body for the first time living inside yourself. Allow your mind to travel to every area of your being. To the tips of your fingers and toes, through your muscles, bones, and organs. Feel your heartbeat and the circulation coursing through you. Be in the full experience of self.

Now bring your awareness to your closed eyelids, and you look into the darkness of space. Feel the sensation of the vastness that space offers you and how ever-expanding it is. As you continue to breathe in and out, feel your body's energy expand into this vastness, so you become more prominent and greater than you already are.

Bring your awareness into the space of your third eye between your eyebrows. You will be watching through the lens of the higher self, which is all-knowing, giving, and receiving. The images will appear to you like watching a movie on a big screen in a dark empty theater. You will feel all emotions and sensations as you observe yourself move through this practice.

See yourself standing under the light of a full moon, in a grassy null. The air is warm and dry. Your body is comfortable. The sky is bright from the light of the luminescent moon shining down upon you. You take a deep breath in and feel a sense of wholeness in your body.

Beneath your feet, you feel a pulse from the earth. The womb of Mother Earth beckons you to release your pain to her. Mother earth is all-powerful. She can transform energy.

You begin to use your hands and fingers to dig into the warm loose soil. You are digging a hole just big enough to plant your very own seed.

Once the hole is ready, you rise, standing firm, healthy, and free. Reaching your arms to the sky, you receive the bounty from the light of the moon. She energizes you as she bathes you in her light. Luna is comfort, sensuality, primal, and powerful.

Reaching deep inside your energetic body and extracting the seed of pain that was embedded in you a long time ago. This seed contains all thoughts, images, feelings, emotions, and memories of every wrongdoing.

You feel the life you have given these wounds vibrating in your hand. Kneeling, you give this seed of wounds and pain back to Mother Earth. You are burying it deep inside of her.

She receives your pain and takes it as her own. Deep into the earth, it is sent where she will transform it.

A shower of light dances over you, and as it hits the ground, the earth becomes moist. You feel a rumbling of the earth beneath your feet, knowing your Mother is doing her work. As you take your next breath in you, see pushing through the soil, a strong sprout of green bearing a small pod. Up, up, up it reaches towards the silver moon and opens into the most beautiful white flower you have ever seen. This flower is you; it began as the energy of pain and used that energy to transform into the truth. Pain has transformed into beauty, wounds into healing. A single flower is swaying in the light breeze, ever reaching towards the light and always representing the beauty and love that is who you indeed are.

When you are ready, come back to your even slow breath. Observe your body free and flowing full of positive energy. Grab your journal and begin to free write your revelations during this meditation. Do not discount any thoughts, feelings, or emotions; everything you experienced has meaning and is vital for your progress.

Come back to this mediation throughout this week of learning about your **"What."** With each practice, new insight is offered. Continue to journal what you have learned about yourself. With each exercise, you will observe yourself releasing more pain and expanding into the most fantastic version of yourself!

Gratitude:

For the practice of Gratitude, list all you are grateful for from this week's meditation practice. It is good to retouch the feelings you just went through with the mediation practice. With each day in this practice, you will release many wounds' energy and gain more clarity. At the end of your week of **"What,"** you will be able to see all you have let go of and gained.

Week Three: When

Diving into your "When" hurts; it is uncomfortable and, by far, is the hardest part of the journey. Your "When" is the meat of your transformation! Be brave! Rember, I have you through this. My thoughts, prayers, and intentions are that you are observing old wounds and finding peace through the work. Thoughts are powerful. Thoughts are the armor that we wear, and that armor will either protect us or hinder us.

There are many **"When's"** in our lives. We will focus on two types, the past, and the not so distant past, for this week's journey. The **"When"** from childhood, and the **"When"** from adulthood. Our **"When"** defines the story you have written about your life. It is **"When"** you identify the trauma, as it left an indelible mark on us, and from a cellular level, it created energy of defining how we relate to the world around us.

We are all not without trauma. Trauma has created a program of thought and action that has caused us to define ourselves unknowingly through the events that happened in our lives. This definition of self did not come knowingly; for most, it was through Fight or Flight that the body processed pain. You either fight or flee.

It was not until I was 47 years old that I truly acknowledged how I dealt with the traumas in my life. I understood what I was doing, but the light bulb of truth did not fully brighten until I owned that I was inevitably repeating the same manifestation of my experiences. Ironically it was through the process of writing this book that I recognized many of my patterns.

Understanding the fight or flight response is beneficial, and I encourage you if you are not familiar with fight or flight to further educate yourself on it. The discovery of self is continually evolving; it will always be a work in progress. Through each practice, we learn and grow. The work you accomplish here is just the first stepping stone in many lifelong self-evolution stages.

Let's begin by hitting the rewind button in your subconscious mind. Rember this is uncomfortable, and please be gentle with yourself as you marinate in your hard memories. You may even be feeling like you just want to close this book now and walk away. Trust me, I understand. I can't tell you how many times I have stared at the blank page, not writing this chapter. Even at the moment now that I write this, I feel very sick and uncomfortable. I am holding your hand here; I am right here with you, I promise! We will start gingerly, slowly peeling back the thinnest layers. This part will not get done in one sitting, but if you can dedicate to yourself at least one hour each day this week to answer these questions, there will be a great movement of energy. Unraveling with compassion allows us to view all events in our life from a clear lens. As if you are watching your life from afar, you can observe what has happened and lovingly address yourself. Observation is a significant part of gaining self-love. When you can observe your past without judgment, work within the context of what has happened to you, and your choices, then my friends' healing begins. It's time to reflect.

- **When in your memory, can you recall feeling alone? Journal a detailed description of this feeling. Maybe it was an actual event or overall energy that hovered like a cloud in your life. Be descriptive; bring yourself right back to that time and place. Feel it fully without judgment. Just be in the moment with your emotions.**

- **When in your life have you felt shame? List 8 occurrences that brought you to feelings of guilt?**

- **When in your childhood, were you told or experienced that you were not worthy of happiness, success, and love? List all times you felt unworthy of these things.**

- **When was the first time as an adult that you experienced pain that resulted in victimization behavior?**

- **When were you able to identify the patterns of toxic behaviors resulting from the first assault of pain, shame, and abuse in your life?**

These are not comfortable areas of your life to explore. Breathe and remember that you are the soul energy of love. It is my personal belief that our soul has a contract with Divine Source. This contract guided our soul to choose a life that will give us experiences to learn and grow from, so eventually, we may ascend to a higher level of consciousness. I completely acknowledge that I have spent all of my life with a victim mentality. This realization is not an energy that I have been working on for long. It was not until I dove deep into reflection, choosing to become incredibly uncomfortable. I saw that I created a personality of victimization through my lack of self-worth. Though some out of my control, the wrongdoings that happened in my life paved a brokenness pathway as an adult. Breaking the paths of thought takes awareness and discipline. We become that which we think and feel. We operate from a habit of thinking. It is not your fault that you repeated patterns of behaviors. It is your programming. Hopefully, with this newfound awareness, you will take the opportunity that is given to you here to create a new path. Again, this is merely a small step in the journey, but the practice you will develop here is a gift and will benefit you by making you stronger physically and emotionally.

Let's turn the page now to energy of positivity. Life was not all doom and gloom. It is in the joyous moments that we can draw awareness of strength and perseverance! For me, however, finding the positivity in my life was a painful process and realization. After answering these questions myself, I had discovered that the love and support I needed as a child did not come until I was an adult. The support and nurturing I yearned for arrived later in teachers, mentors, and friends. It is excruciating to sit in the absence of love. However, it is here that you can find forgiveness and compassion! —Journal through these next few observations with grace and understanding that you are ok!

- **When was the first time you witness someone supporting you unconditionally?**

- **When was the first time you remember experiencing unconditional love?**

- **List five memories when you felt love and accepted.**

- **When have you experienced pure joy?**

A little something about forgiveness:

If you are anything like me, acknowledging the positive times you were supported and loved was not easy. For many of us, childhood was no walk in the park! It may be that you discovered that your parents or caregivers abandoned most of your foundational years emotionally, leaving you unsupported in many ways. Hopefully, this was not the case for you, but it is in many instances for many people. Forgiveness is a critical element in the process of transformation. It wasn't until I learned about Yoga's tenants that I indeed could adopt a forgiving mind.

Yoga has been one of my most outstanding teachers. Yoga has given me the tools to observe my experiences from a lens of non-judgment. Forgiveness falls under an important rule. In Sanskrit, the word Aparigraha means to "let go."

As I practice forgiveness, I slowly let go of the pain and resentment I felt from early choices made for me. I found the strength to ask the hard why questions. The adage is true; you can not fully love someone else until you love yourself! Now, as an adult, I work on loving myself every single day! The most significant reason why is so I can love my children to the utmost capacity. Secondly, I desire freedom within!

Personal Story:

Rehashing the events of our lives is challenging and painful. But in our memories, we can identify the stories of victimization we have been telling ourselves for a lifetime. We can find the strength to let go of our victimization. You can probably account for endless stories of emotional abandonment, abuse, humiliation, and terror. There are lessons to be learned in all of them. Living through them all is unnecessary, but reflecting on the energy of pain they created is essential.

In my life now, I keep myself accountable for my choices. My core values determine my decision-making, and I try my best to live by them daily.

Deep within my childhood years were acts of sexual abuse, emotional abandonment, shaming, and humiliation. The perpetrators of these acts were family members and people in the community in which we lived. I felt alone emotionally, and as I grew into a young woman, I yearned for love and acceptance. As I look back on those moments now, I can see how desperately I needed and wanted love and affection. Had I felt safe as a child, the program that became my lens would have wired differently.

Now it is time to reflect upon the answers to the questions above. Think about how you have grown and what you are learning from your discoveries.

Mission Statement:

For this Mission Statment, think about how much you have learned from identifying When you felt pain, loss, and confusion. Recognize how well you have come through these challenging times. Pay tribute to the times in your life when those you loved supported you. As you enter into this new chapter of awareness and transformation, describe how you will command into your life energy of success when you need it most.

"I _____ When feeling most vulnerable, I will remember my inner strengths. When I feel weak, I will remind myself that I can transform my thoughts into action for success. When I feel alone, I will bring into my awareness all the joy my life has provided for me!"

For the sake of your development, it would be a good idea to print your mission statements and place them around your home, car, office, and anywhere you spend your time. Your ego will want to bring you into isolation often. Overriding your habits of thought takes daily work. Give yourself a boost each day by reading your mission statement and proclaiming your success!

Asana:

The posture I have chosen for this next stage in your transformation is "Bidalasana" otherwise known as "Cat/Cow" Pose. Personally, this posture is by far my most favorite asana to practice. This posture offers a sense of grounding as well as opening and expanding through the heart. It is a perfect combination of being rooted in the earth and saying yes to the universe! There is also a sense in this posture of feeling raw and primal. When practiced with the eyes closed, Cat/Cow connects you deeply with the root chakra. With the breath, this posture relaxes the body but can also be very energizing!

It is good to have a yoga mat to practice Bidalasana. As I have mentioned earlier, your mat becomes your safe space. It creates a boundary for your energy to live within. If you allow it, your yoga mat can become a home for you.

The Practice of Bidalasana: Cat/Cow pose

To begin in Cat/Cow pose, find yourself on all fours on your mat. Palms of your hands down, knees on the mat, top of the feet if possible flat to the ground. You want to have your knee's hip-width distance apart, your wrists stacked underneath your shoulders. Be careful not to hyperflex your writs in this position. Hollow out the palm of your hands by pressing into the finger pads of your palms. Send your gaze to the top of your mat. Feel the length of your spine as you Spend a few moments like this, connecting to your breath. Feel your inhalation and exhalation. Notice any areas you may be holding tension, especially in your face and shoulders, and direct your breath to relax your muscles. Relax your jaw, and drop your tongue from the roof of your mouth.

Let's begin to move now. Drop your belly as you inhale, expanding your collar bone. Imagine your collar bone as a big happy smile expanding to the sun! You do this by drawing your shoulder blades close together. Imagine holding a pencil between your shoulders. Squeezing your shoulders as you feel the weight of your belly reaches towards the earth. Cow pose is fully open and exposed. Your heart beams outward as you breathe in.

Moving into Cat pose, imagine you are pressing the earth away through the palms of your hands as you exhale. Your breath is exiting your body. Your abdomen will contract and pull toward your spine with your exhalation, your tailbone tucks in, and your spine arches. Tuck your chin towards your chest.

Inhale your belly fills, your collar bone expands, exhale your belly contracts your spine is arched, chin towards the chest. Repeat this with your eyes closed. Be in the moment; feel your breath as it moves through your body. Notice any thoughts, feelings, or emotions that may appear as you move through this posture. Do not label or judge what you see in your mind or feel emotionally in your body.

Inhale Cow pose
Exhale Cat pose
Inhale Cow pose
Exhale Cat pose
Move through this rhythm for 15 breaths.

To exit out of this posture, take a moment in Childs Pose "Balasana."

Press your sit bones towards your heels, allowing your forehead to seek the mat if you are able. Reach your fingertips towards the top of your mat—arm variations to your comfort and flexibility. Arms can rest gently by your side, and palms face up, arms may be extended in front of you resting on the mat or for a more active variation, lift the forearms off the mat. Arms also may stack in front of your face resting your forehead on them. Sink in here for a few breaths.

Meditation:

For this meditation, the "When" we are focusing on is vulnerability. "When" you are vulnerable, you are open and exposed. We may receive messages and guidance that our armor may not let us see in other circumstances. Armor being our ego, predominantly our fear.

I love meditation because when practiced, we have a direct entrance into the subconscious mind! Remember the toddler that lives in your mind? The subconscious believes everything you tell it! It is why you hear so many stories of people healing themselves of life-threatening diseases through thought. The "Power" of thought is not just a New-Age Movement. The power of thought is the one fundamental element of your life that you absolutely can control. There is no single person in the world who governs what you think, therefore nor do they have a say over what you feel. Since thoughts create feelings, which then make energy, you and you alone are the master of your mind!

As I mentioned, my connection to my Source has completely inspired this book. That is why I believe in the healing power of these meditations. When practiced repeatedly, I believe the words that are channeled from Spirit through me are meant to help you rewire your mind towards healing! When I facilitate these meditations, I ask Spirit to please give the reader a session to heal their minds and bodies. These meditations are a gift and should be held deeply in your heart as such. The love you feel to receive them will only enhance your transformation experience.

Let's begin with our meditation.

Dear one, you only need to relax, trust and believe in the possibilities of letting go.

Find a comfortable place to sit or lie down uninterrupted for the next 20 minutes. I would like you to relax here profoundly, so please be as cozy and comfortable as you possibly can. Blankets and pillows are encouraged. If you have added props, a bolster for under your knees, a weighted blanket or sandbag an eye pillow, please indulge. Dim your lights, and let's begin.

Deep, deep in your past before you came to this vibrational plane, your soul existed in its true form, brilliant light of energy. This energy is your soul, which is encoded with knowledge from many lifetimes. This energy is supreme; it is love.

Before you chose to descend into the vibrational field of the earth, taking on your human form, you made a decision. You decided to endure pain, anguish, discomfort, and for some, there was a decision to suffer. Since You decided to experience pain, you also have chosen the experiences of pleasure, happiness, peace, and contentment. You see, without experiencing the feelings that fear produces, you would never understand joy. When you are in your proper form of light, you do not fear. You know and understand the lessons you must learn and take them on with conviction and courage. You, dear one, have chosen every minute of your life's experience. You are incredibly brave, whether you believe it or not!

Take a long deep inhale into your abdomen. Feel the coolness of your inhalation as it enters your body. Notice you exhale, warm as it leaves you.

Long deep inhale, Long deep exhale.

Soften your jaw, release your tongue from the roof of your mouth.

Encourage all tension areas you are aware of in your body to soften as you sink into relaxation.

At this moment, you have all that you need. There is nothing to worry about, nothing to do, nowhere to go. This moment is for you to receive the healing your body and mind so desperately desires.

I want you now to see yourself standing as light. Do not label or judge this experience. Do not try to manipulate it. Remember that all inspired thought comes from your higher self, which means it comes from love.

Embodied as light, you are standing at the top of a very steep staircase. At the bottom, all you can see is luminescent light filling all four corners of a room. This white light is brightly shining as you begin to descend one careful step at a time.

With each step, you feel a heaviness in your feet that anchors you. You feel balanced; your entire body is vibrating with the flow of energy coursing through you.

As you reach the bottom of the staircase, you notice before you a wooden table. Illuminated by light, you see atop the table an intricate wooden box. Inside this box is all the pain you have ever experienced in your life. Do not fear or hesitate. Remember you have already lived this; you are all-knowing, and all are receiving. Opening this box, you will experience all the emotions that have hurt you from your past. This experience, however, is different than the first time you lived these events. In this experience, you view your pain from awakened eyes and a whole heart. You experience the pain from a place of gratitude for all you have learned, having already lived through it; you are full of knowledge, compassion, and understanding.

Taking a deep breath in, feel the comfort of the light surrounding you. Innately, you are feeling the love of Source bathing your entire being. As you view the events from your life path, you are reminded that though these experiences have at one time caused pain; now you are healed and free. You look upon these experiences as lessons; your heart fills with gratitude for them and all those involved. You gaze upon these events with forgiveness and love. You see, the enlightened soul you now does not hold attachment to the pain of the past. You that is pure light energy is finally free.

Take a deep breath in, place your hands over your heart space, and smile. At this moment, you are complete. You remember who you are, pure light. You recall your soul's decision to enter into this life, and you feel peace for your journey.

Before returning to the physical space you are in, you gently close the box containing your memories, offering them to the universe as a sign of your ascension to your next level of awareness. You have exposed your darkest secrets, your greatest shame, your deepest pain, and in doing so, you have let go. The cord attaching you to the past has been severed. The work is complete.

Come back to your breath. Come back to your physical body. Come back to yourself.

Remember to continue to practice this mediation throughout the week. With each practice, you will find revelation as you release layers of shame, guilt, and pain. Return to your "When" questions, contemplate them as you move through this week with greater awareness.

Gratitude:

You have just traveled through an incredible journey of realization. Within the corners of your mind, you discovered yourself. Your vulnerability exposes the truth within, therefore allowing you to ascend to a higher state of awareness. Congratulations! For this, you should feel grateful and proud.

For this practice of Gratitude, the exercise is nurturing and fruitful. We are at a turning point in your transformation. Hopefully, you are beginning to see your thoughts' patterns and how you can quickly transform them through daily rituals and practice!

You are sowing the seeds to a fruitful future! A future that will lead you to even greater levels of enlightenment and happiness. This work may be your first venture in discovering who you really are and who you are truly meant to be. Transformation is a continuous journey. This may not be the first attempt at healing. For many, though, it serves as a platform to begin.

To celebrate in Gratitude your new beginning, becoming vulnerable, and accepting yourself finally as a force of energy meant to experience pain and joy, I feel it appropriate to represent Gratitude in planting your seeds of change.

Part of the transformation process is self-care. Self-care is what you have been doing the last few weeks as you follow the daily rituals in this book. There are many ways to love yourself! In my opinion, small gestures of love have the most significant impact on energy.

You will need to carve out some time this week for this part of the practice.

Carefully choose a planting pot. When I say carefully, I mean with great love and care for what brings you happiness. Personally, my gratitude pot is brightly painted with mosaics full of color, vibrant and happy!

You will be planting your Gratitude to represent the life that it gives.

Choose your indoor houseplant carefully. Part of your self-care is taking the time to research the meaning of the plant, what type of environment it needs to live sustainably in your home, one that will bring you great pleasure when you view it and care for it feelings of love. Your plant will be a representation of all that you have accomplished. Each stage of its growth as it pushes up out of the dark soil reminds you of your journey from darkness to light!

For this project, you will also need a few small pieces of paper and a pen.

Planting day should be a ceremony. Once again, like all components of this practice, you should be alone with no distractions. If the time of year serves or the climate is optimal, it is best to perform this gratitude ceremony under the moon's light, in nature barefoot in the grass. However, these conditions are not necessary for success; they merely add energetically more force to the ceremony.

On your pieces of paper, list five things you are currently grateful for. These things should align with your journey, a representation of your awareness around your transformation and healing. Take your time to examine your heart. What does your heart tell you at the moment? Make it count! The frequencies that are our thoughts are potent. These vibrations magnify as we take them out of your mind into action, from there into something tangible. For this, you are giving your thoughts life.

Once made, you will now list five things you are grateful for coming into your existence. Yes, you read this correctly. You will manifest these experiences into your life because you have changed your belief system to that of limitless possibility! No longer does your mind follow the track of lack! With continued practice, your mind is a co-creator with your heart! What life does your heart desire? Without fear, without doubt, without anyone or anything getting in the way? "Where" do you see yourself in the next five years? "Where" are you and "What" are you doing? List these five things and be descriptive. There is no limit to what you can accomplish!

Once listed, it is time to perform your Gratitude ritual. Seeds, soil, intentions, love all waiting to be planted.

Prepare your planting pot by filling it halfway with soil. Fold each paper into a small ball, and gather your seeds and lists into the palm of your hand. With one hand over the other palm, repeat this affirmation as it comes from Spirit!

"With a clear mind and a healthy heart, I command,
my dreams, I will not let fear tear me apart."

Repeat 10x as you place your seeds and lists into the soil.

As your Gratitude plant begins to sprout, the energy it omits will feed your soul. Your Gratitude plant is a pleasant reminder of how much you have healed and what is yet to come!

Where:

You have gone the distance; you know where you were and where you want to be. You recognize the hard work it takes to look into yourself to discover the truth, and finally, after all this time, begin the process of transformation!

To discover your "Where," you must stand on the edge of truth as you know it and retrieve the memories of the past. Identifying you're "Where" may, for some be very easy; we know and replay that one event that changed the course of our lives over and over again. For some, there is a defining moment in life where the pain is so intense that we have no other alternative but to take action. Your "Where" may be a physical place in your life, or it could merely have been the perspective you had at any given moment in time that left an indelible mark upon you. For me, it was both. Where I was in life, and where my heart cried out to be for many years.

Where were you, and where are you now? Don't think things have changed that much? Really? I will bet you were not thinking of self-actualization and transformation when you were in the darkest moments of your life. You have come much farther than you think you have! You may not believe it, but you HAVE turned lemons into lemonade more times than you can count. You had no other means of coping than by pushing on. That is ok! When I think about where I was in life when I had no other choice to make a change, the first thing that comes to my mind is where my heart resided. During my adult life's most significant trauma, it was not the event that pushed me to find my courage, but the pure exhaustion that my heart had experienced. Whether you like it or not, change is going to happen. It will come from you being proactive with clarity and conviction, or it will merely arrive like a tremendous tornado sweeping through your life, causing devastation everywhere it touches. Your repetitive thoughts determine this. Once again, until you discipline yourself to change your program, your thoughts inevitably will create your reality. It is the law of the universe to do so! The good news is you are here, and you are working within yourself! If you have made it this far, you have spent the last month peeling away at that nasty onion called life. You have uncovered some hard-hitting truths about your life and your decision-making, and you are still going—time to dig harder. It feels raw, I know. I have stood on the edge of my truth so many times and have walked away. I have made excuses, lived in denial, and turned my back on what was before me. In the end, I have landed where you are now, right back where I started. We must follow through if we want to love ourselves. We must experience completion. There is a reason why.

For transformation to happen, there must be space for you to transform. Remember that everything is energy. Our thoughts are energy, the pain we feel is energy, our emotions and the actions or inaction that we take is energy and all of that energy takes up a ton of space in our lives! The success you will feel when adapting a pure and unconditional love for yourself has its unique strength. That energy needs space to sprout, grow, and expand. You must remove the lower energies from your field so that the higher vibrations of love can exist! Reflect upon the questions about your "**Where.**" answer without fear, be brave as you look at those moments in space and times that caused you the most pain.

- **Where were you in your life when you were forced to make a physical change?**

- **Where in your childhood, did you feel powerless?**

- **Where in your adulthood did the energy of victimization determine your choices?**

- **Where do you feel the most emotional and physical pain?**

Take your time. Reflect, and let your memory carry you back even though it hurts. Remember, this is about letting go and gaining love, self-love! I have come to discover many times in reflection on these very questions that the answers change. When we start working on the trauma, we heal the energy of the open emotional wounds. With observation, disciplined practice in self-love and forgiveness, we release the events energetically. We can never fully erase what has happened in time, but we can close the past's energetic wounds.

- **How did your friends, loved ones, co-workers, family show up for you during the most vulnerable times of your life?**

- **In your childhood/adolescence, list five times you felt loved and worthy.**

- **As an adult, list five times you felt loved and worthy?**

- **List 5 choices you made throughout your life that made you feel empowered and in control.**

- **When dealing with emotional or physical pain, list a time when you relied on the wisdom of your higher-self for guidance.**

Trust the process of vulnerability. There is nothing revealed or healed behind the closed doors of the mind. Shame is very comfortable locked away. It is not easy revealing who shamed you to yourself because it is usually the closest people to us. For some of us, our parents were abusive and treated us terribly. For some, our parents were unknowingly operating from their broken places. Forgive. Forgive because it free's you. Forgive because your pent up anger and sadness affect other people. Forgive because you want to experience self-love!

Over the years, I have heard many students say that they wish to forgive those who have wronged them, but they do not know-how. I wish I had a magic wand for forgiveness. If I could bless everyone with the ability to forgive, I would instantly! Forgiveness takes work, discipline, and the desire to experience true freedom, separation of the ego. The ego has a job; it wants to keep you safe. From the time you were small, it has protected you. As we grow, the ego then becomes the very thing we fight. Only with observation can we see its hindrance. Ego says I will keep you safe. The only real truth is that you are constructed from the energy of love. This love reveals to you that you are and always have been safe. Nothing, no power on earth or beyond, can penetrate, harm, or destroy love. You are love! The ego can, however, manipulate love.

For this reason, we work within ourselves to override the ego and let the love that is you shine! Forgiveness is a powerful tool in living your authentic life. If you practice forgiveness, you are feeding your soul as you set your mind and body free. Setting intentions to forgive and commanding thoughts of forgiveness in your yoga and meditation practice is a direct path to freedom of the ego.

A Personal Story:

"Girl, it took the Lord to burn down your house to get you to leave this life, now you get up and go!" These words echo in my mind whenever I think about my exit back to myself. They came days after losing my home to a tragedy, only days after Christmas in 2012. I found myself in the arms of an old southern woman weeping as I told the story of how desperate my life had become. Terrified is a mild adjective to describe what I was feeling. I had no means to support my family. My home was gone, no possessions, only my dignity and the rawness of rock bottom. There was no fight in me left. My life broke me to pieces, and I was in a fog.

Betrayal, in my opinion, causes extraction of self. When someone you love betrays you, your ability to comprehend the wrongdoing is overshadowed by the deep well of shame, regret, pain, and loss you are experiencing. Fear becomes your compass. Betrayal hits the very depths of your heart, leaving emotional wounds that only forgiveness will allow you to overcome.

There was no other option; I had to leave. I needed to retreat to the only place I knew. I had no idea what was next. I was in the moment more than I had ever been in my life. I only knew I needed to go. Not for any other reason but to be free. My youngest son was six months old, my middle Son 3, my oldest 8.

I recall feeling so exhausted like there was no life left in me at all. I was on autopilot. I just knew I had to get from point A to point B safely.

The morning I left my life, was dark, wet, and cold. The journey would be rough, with children crying, a baby needing to nurse every two hours, and all the things a challenging journey entails. I was alone, so alone. I can still see my home as I drove away from it, knowing I would never step foot inside the life I worked so hard at creating: busted windows, holes in the roof, soot-covered exterior. Peering inside, one could only see darkness. The inside was a nightmare that raged in my reality. My home was where I nursed my babies, fed them, danced with them, laughed, and cried. Every detail of that house was from the energy I put into it. The walls I painted, the food I cooked, the life I gave to it. The walls of my home contained the love and dreams I had for my family. It was a representation of hope; as I drove away that dark, cold morning, I sobbed a pain so deep it has taken me years to recover.

I wouldn't say I have genuinely healed because I am forever a student of life. I have forgiven, I have held the journey in a place of light and love, and I have more than anything discovered my part in it all. I and I alone created a life with someone who did not love me. I chose to have children and fight for that life regardless of the emotional abandonment I endured. I am no longer concerned about the details or the events that brought us to the day I pulled away from the only life I knew. What concerns me most is why I chose to invest for so long in a life where I was unloved.

There are lessons to be learned in reflecting. I will always love the person I know once existed. I will continue to hold a place of light and forgiveness for the reality that was once my life. I once read that inflicting pain is the soul's way of loving another. I believe the pain I went through was a lesson taught from one soul to another. That belief is a salve for my deep wounds of sorrow. True healing comes from forgiveness, and forgiveness came from realizing why I attracted an unhealthy relationship and stayed for as long as I did. Now years later, I continue to embody the light of forgiveness. I welcome healing, friendship, and acceptance. I am finally free of needing approval, desperately wanting love, and requiring attention. There is freedom in forgiveness.

We begin in the now. In the now, all we have is "**Where**" we are! It is vital to define where you are. Where you are is not where anyone else is going ever to be. Where you are is your starting point and your landing point. We must know where we are to begin, and where we are every day is different. As we practice, we grow, expand our energy, always evolve, ascend, and heighten our vibrations! Here is where things get interesting and exciting. There is so much peace when we realize why we made the decisions we made in our lives! The discovery of the program we operate from, which directs our choices, is the biggest "aha" moment you can experience. This discovery is enlightening and removes the mountain of guilt and shame you carry.

It took doing the work, diving into the questions to discover why I chose the life I lived. As I journaled the answers to my questions, I learned about my childhood. My memories opened the door to who, what, when, where, and why your programs of thought were put into place. Think about the word "journal" to journal is to "journey" into self. Yes! In my journaling practice, or otherwise labeled my practice in reflection, I could see the large holes of love missing from my life. In doing my hard work, I discovered a hard truth, the most freeing realization I have ever had. I choose my past life because I wanted to be successful. I did not love myself enough to believe I could ever be whole without someone else's success by my side.

For me, success meant home, family, and successful marriage. Through the years, my marriage should have ended countless times. It was me who always came running back. The emotional pain, the shaming, was my addiction. Living in a toxic pit of hopelessness was my drug. Why? Because I hated myself. I hated myself; I could never do enough or be good enough was my perception.

I threw myself full force into a relationship that I thought would define me as significant. If I was loved, I would be worthy. If I could create a prosperous family, I would be someone important. I gave every ounce of myself to someone else's success because, in my mind, I was not worthy of winning on my own.

When I first left my life, a dear friend of mine said to me, "Shannon, if you truly want to heal, own your part in this." For many years I owned that I turned my head to all the wrongdoing. I realize now that I must acknowledge that I chose that life, and my part was my acceptance in allowing myself to be a victim. As victims, we are not responsible for our choices; we tell a story about what has happened to us, pointing to blame outside of ourselves! I stand firmly now in the conviction that what happened to me was my own doing! I chose to stay! The victimization was my manifestation of the program I was choosing to live out throughout my life. Like an addict needing a drug, my drug was self-hatred. The chemicals inside my brain sought out experiences that would feed my addictive behavior of not loving myself. This behavior manifested into my horrible actualization of unrequited love.

Wherever you are in your life right now, it is essential to reconnect with your heart. Your heart center is the space where forgiveness is born. Let's move on now to taking action with the new-found knowledge you have gained. Remember to come back to your questions throughout the week as you unravel the truth to yourself.

Mission Statement:

"Where ever I am in life, I acknowledge that I can always begin again. I am right where I am supposed to be to rise and climb. Where I was is a lesson in forgiveness and self-love. I am stronger than I realize, and I will use my strength as a marker to begin again!"

Please feel free to use my mission statement or create your own. This powerful affirmation will carry you when you feel weak and ignite you when you feel powerful!

Asana:

"Virabhadrasana 1," otherwise known as Warrior 1. This strong-rooted posture grounds us as we open the heart with Goddess Arms!

Virabhadrasana 1: Warrior One Pose

To begin, stand at the top of your yoga mat with your feet hip-width distance apart. Bring your attention to your breath. Soften your jaw, release your tongue from the roof of your mouth. Soften the muscles of your face. Feel the souls of your feet connected to the earth, feel the vibrational energy of the earth move through you as you inhale. As you exhale, free yourself by letting go of any unwanted thoughts, feelings, or emotions. Soften your shoulders down your back, tuck your tailbone, and feel the strength of your quadriceps like the roots of a tree.

With your next inhalation, raise your arms above your head, reach for the sky, and bring your hands down to pray.

Root down into your left leg; imagine your left leg filled with sand it is strong and sturdy. Slowly begin to lift your right knee towards your chest; as you do so, send your right foot to the back of your mat, dropping it down at a 45-degree angle (big toe headed towards the top right corner of the mat).

Now let's align!

Place your hands on your hips.

Track your left knee in line with your second and third toes of your left foot.

Draw your right hip back and your left hip forward as you tuck your tailbone and neutralize your pelvis.

Look down at your feet. The heel of your front foot should line up with the soul of your back foot.

Once anchored strongly here, raise your arms towards the sky for one breath and then slowly position your arms in the shape of goalposts bringing your pointer finger and thumb together.

Slightly arch your spine and shine your heart space forward!

You are broadening your collarbone as you breathe, drawing your shoulders towards each other.

With each inhale, imagine a beautiful golden light shining from your heart space! Beams of light bursting from your heart! This light is your truth. Sink into this posture for ten breaths. You will begin to feel a burn in your shoulders; this is ok, it's your lifeforce, your "prana" reminding you you are alive!

Observe what images rise with the burn in your body. What is released from your mind? Where do you want to go? How deep will you sink into yourself?

When you are ready to exit out of the posture, bring your hands back to the prayer position. Step your back foot to the front of your mat.

Fold forward and let your body be a ragdoll here.

Meditation:

Do this meditation in Savasana, or any comfortable position is lying down. Dress warm and cozy, support your body with any props that will help your muscles relax.

This meditation is channeled healing for your inner child. It Induces an experience of being in the womb, leading your consciousness back to a place where you felt safe and secure. If white noise is available, please use it to enhance this meditative experience. Spirit is waiting to envelop you in love.

Place both hands over your heart as you slow your breath. Long deep inhale, long deep exhale. Feel your heartbeat—the pulse of life beating against the palm our your hand. The muscle of your heart wants you to be free. Your heart channels life through you, all that you are can be found within the energy of your heart.

Deep within your subconscious mind are the imprints of the months you lived as one with your Mother. Her body fed you; her breath brought oxygen to you; her heartbeat was the music that bathed your experience in her womb. See yourself in her womb connected to her.

Now bring your awareness to your feet, feel the energy of warmth surrounding your feet. Notice this warmth as the color pink surrounding you. Every cell in your body responds to this healing energy. Breath in and feel this warmth begin to travel up your legs, around your knees, over and under your thighs, and surrounding your pelvis.

Take a deep full belly breath in and pull this loving energy up around your abdomen, chest, and shoulders...encasing your arms, and finally your head.

Feel the vibration of love all around you. This same loving energy was the blanket of love that caressed you living within the womb of your mother. Feel it's nurturing life as you rest peacefully in it now. Every cell in your body seeks this love and responds to it, feeding you at this moment.

Everywhere you have ever been physically and emotionally in your life has always been carried by this loving energy. Though at times you may not have felt it, it was still present and alive. This energy comes from the divinity of your soul and is your birthright. It is imprinted in your energetic body and will never leave you; it is the truth of who you are.

Your soul will always remember every moment of its life in your body. Just as your memory serves you in this consciousness, there is a memory imprinted in your soul's energy. Your soul is the energy of the Divine; there is no separation. Just as your umbilical cord connected you to your mothers' physical body, so does the power of love connect you to your source maker.

Everything that you need to lead a fulfilling, peaceful life in your everyday experience resides within this beautiful energy of love.

Take a full belly breath in as you draw this energy consciously into your physical body. See the loving pink energy entering into you as it travels through your cells, muscles, organs, and to any area in need of healing.

You have never left the safety of your Mothers womb; the energy has transformed and lives inside of you.

Continue to inhale and exhale fully, feeling your body heavy and relaxed. Stay in this position for as long as you are able. Don't worry if you drift off to sleep; your body is in a state of relaxation, happy and peaceful. Marinate here for as long as you are able.

Gratitude Practice:

This practice of gratitude is to follow your mediation immediately. As you do the following mediation over each day, observe how this gratitude practice offers an awakening to the abundance of love in your life.

For this practice, you will need colored pencils, markers, or crayons. You can either use your journal for paper or designate a sketch pad for this particular work. I like to have my expressions of gratitude in a specific place just for my artistic expression. I use a small sketch pad to doodle—this practice is an opportunity to express appreciation and is also meditative. Don't worry if you are not an artist, only you will see it. Look upon it without judgment. It is growth and a beautiful way of expression in a not so conventional form.

Take a few moments to think about your experience in your meditation. What images come to your mind when you reflect? Maybe it's the image of your Mother or you as a baby living in her womb. Perhaps these images take on different forms representing your experience. Whatever comes to your mind, allow yourself to be free in your expression as you draw your thankfulness. Think of these drawings as a gift—a gift to yourself and the universe. Whatever flows through you is part of your transformation. It is an honest expression of your love for yourself!

Each time you do the above mediation this week, follow it with your gratitude expression through art. You may find great relaxation in revealing how you are transforming into a more fantastic version of yourself!

Week Four: Why

Wow! Look how far you have come!

First I have to say, congratulations! It is a considerable accomplishment to stick to any program, especially one that requires you to not only make physical changes but forces you to buckle down and take the ride back to your authentic self! Maybe you did not practice every day, that is ok, be kind to yourself. Wherever you are on this journey is yours. This practice is only going where you lead it. It will always be waiting for you when you are ready to embark! It is hard enough to practice yoga every day, significantly if you do not move that much and did not have an active lifestyle before this. I hope you feel the benefits of opening your body through yoga practice. And the expansion and transformation of the mind through the daily disciplines of exploring yourself in this work. The exercises detailed throughout the program are given to support your evolution of self and is my belief to be tools to transform. If you have followed through with each exercise, you should by now notice you are not the same! Your transformation through this process is "**WHY**" you have shown up for yourself every day of this journey! I am so excited for you! You are in the home stretch! Before we move on, give yourself a great big hug, do a little dance, and smile! Hello you! This new person you are feeling is closer to understanding self-love than you were a month ago! I am sure it feels amazing! Now let's get back to work. There is one week left and still much to do. Let's talk about **WHY**.

If you have worked this program to it's fullest, you should have some answers as to why you have made certain decisions in your life. The actions you have taken and the repetitive thoughts should be evident to you by now. If these things are not clear, I encourage you to go back to parts of the program where you did not fully commit. Remember, we are always beginning every single day. If you have to start again in week one or two or wherever you fell off, do it for the greater good of your happiness!

How many times in life have you sat with your head in your hands, asking, "why me?" If I had a penny for as many times, I have asked well, you know I'd be a very wealthy woman by now! It is the victim mentality that causes us to spiral into our why's of self-pity. I'd like you to recall earlier in practice when you uncovered you're who, what, when, and where. All of the answers should make very clear; you're why!

In preparation to dive into why, go back, reread the answers to your journal reflections. Sit with your answers, breathe them in as you feel the vibration of your perspective as it is now.

- **As you look back on your life choices, how can you own your part in them?**

- **List 5 reasons why you made your most painful life choices.**

- **Your reasons why will change as you become more awakened to your programs. What is the reason today you are choosing awareness?**

- **Your "Why" should be an anchor for you; nothing you can ever tell yourself should be greater than "Why" loving yourself is crucial! What is the reason why loving yourself should always come first in your life?**

A Personal Story:

The day I walked away from my past, was one of the most challenging days I ever had to face, as I was heading into the unknown. I had chosen out of pure survival to walk away from the only life I understood. A life of dependence, shattered self-worth, and isolation. Leaving was an act of faith. As I was loading my children into the car that day—the wind blowing fiercely, hail, rain, and a long journey ahead, I don't recall how I explained why we were leaving to my children. I only remember the feelings deep inside that hurt like no other pain I have ever felt before. Even now, recalling the memories, my stomach aches, and tears stream down my face. I think all of it still, though feeling it is more of empathy for a person who no longer exists. I see the woman I was, and I know what she went through; I don't identify with her anymore. I am not sure I like feeling that separation from my past; sometimes, I question if it is merely my way of coping? It is as if a piece of me has died, a necessary death. Then I return to the abundance of work that I have accomplished. I have transformed myself into someone of worth. I am a Mother who is not projecting onto her children, a teacher who has the wisdom to share, a healer who can touch someone's broken spirit. Through compassion and understanding, I know I am whole.

I had decided to break my trip back home into two days. It was half a day's drive, and there was no way to do it all in one shot. I decided to stay a night with a lifelong friend. I had taken the same route many times and knew exactly how to get there. Here comes the biggest WHY of all. There was a detour, not the kind with signs signaling me another way, but the type that was so loud and clear that I had no other choice but to listen.

In my mind, I heard very clearly in a loud male voice, "Turn now!" it took me aback and I for a moment became confused.

Looking ahead, I could see an onramp in the left-hand land to turn off the highway (the only route in knew). "Turn now, turn now!" In an instant, my hands turned the wheel, and onto the ramp, I went. Exhausted from days of no sleep, a car full of children crying, I felt a moment of fear as my heart was pounding. I did not know where I was going; I just kept driving. At this point, I was about 6 hours into my trip. When I tell you it was like driving straight into hell, it was. My boys were so traumatized, sad, and scared. They said goodbye to their Father that morning and had no idea when they would see him next. I could not answer; all I could do was comfort them and tell them that we would be ok. Earlier that morning, as we sat preparing to leave, my Son, all over three years old, beckoned me, pointing to the tree above him. "Mamma, do you see him?" "See who baby?" "The angel, sitting there." From the time my boys were born, I spoke to them about Angels' protection in our lives. Could it be they were there showing up for us when we needed them the most?

The road I was on lead directly into the mountains, and for the first time in many hours, the car fell silent. All three of my boys fell asleep. It was here in that moment I began to pray. I needed to speak to God out loud in the silence of the moment. It has been eight years; I can still hear the echo of my plea. "Dear God, I know this won't be easy; I don't expect it to be; I only ask that you allow my eyes to stay open to opportunity, let me see what I need to see to survive." At that moment, the gray clouds that blanketed the sky began to part, revealing a blue sky. Through the clouds, a beam of sunlight cast upon the side of the mountain, and before me in magnificent splendor, three wooden crosses stood! I gasped, I could not believe my eyes! Then the voice that spoke earlier spoke again. "Turn on the radio." I reached over and turned the knob; a voice projected towards me, "God is not only with you for your trials; he is with you through your trials." At that moment, I knew everything would be ok.

The Divine energy of Love, call it whatever it is for you, is my "Why." The why that pulled me out of the gutter so many times I have lost count. The why that forces me to push on when my body feels beaten and broken. My why is always reminding me that I deserve a life bigger than my dreams. God, Jah, Jehovah, Love. A name is just a label, a way for our human minds to separate us from the source. The energy that is you that is me that is God is all the same. Nothing in this existence and beyond can alter love. Love is the most indelible reason WHY!

February first, 2020, I entered a hospital emergency room after a night of intense chest pain. I had spent two years struggling with an elevated resting heart rate. My business had expanded; there was a mountain of stress on my shoulders. Still raising my three children alone, the cortisol in my body was in high production. There was little joy left in my life. I was unhappy every day. I had spent two years dealing with very uncomfortable symptoms of anxiety. I had refused medication; I am a Yogi, for goodness sake, and in my mind, had all the tools to deal with my life situation. The problem was, I was not dealing with it! I was not creating balance, and more than anything, my old programs were rising. I still had not conquered the habitual thinking that drew into my reality experiences that would keep me sick. When presented with a conflict, confrontation, and a boatload of added issues, I internalized it in my program. I pressed on in avoidance to cope.

I did not say no, I did not stand up for myself; I did not create a boundary based on self-love and compassion. As a yoga instructor and a meditation teacher, I often spoke to my students about our bodies' need for balance. I delivered great speeches, infused with information on how to listen to the body. I would remind my students that our bodies will whisper for only so long when in need of change. If you go long enough, ignoring the subtle cries from within, there will be no other alternative but to scream! And scream my body did. On February first, 2020, a Pulmonary Embolism and heart attack nearly took my life.

As you can imagine, physical trauma such as this is painful. I won't go into the lengthy description of what I dealt with for months leading up to this life-changing event. But I will say, I am lucky to be alive. The recovery of this was hard and lonely. Only a month later, Covid 19 hit our world. I still had to parent my children; I still had to provide, I still had to press on despite the damage to my lung and the painful recovery of my heart. Breathing was an issue; moving was an issue; living was an issue! The fear of contracting Covid terrified me. With a weakened heart and damaged lungs, it would kill me for sure, or so I thought.

My children were afraid, and to this day, I do not know the effects those months of seeing me so sick will have on them. What I do know is that my life was not meant to end. I made a promise that never again would I compromise myself for the sake of not wanting conflict, change, or out of fear. Moving forward, I would have more courage and would always, always remember that my gift of life is precious and temporary! My higher self speaks to me each day in visions of opportunities. My spirit is alive and excited for a future filled with love and compassion! My why resides anchored in love; and will never be uprooted!

Mission Statement:

"I am granted the gift of life; I seize every opportunity to evolve into the greatest version of myself! I leave the emotions of fear behind as I continue to work on conquering old programs of thought. Loving myself is the most important reason why I work so hard!"

Asana:

Balasana: Childs Pose

Bow and surrender unto yourself. Come vulnerable to your knees and allow the energy to flow through you without resistance!

Though this posture is better known for rest, in practice, it can also be a place one comes to for humility. With head bowed, one can sense the presence of Love all around them. There is no place for ego here, only acceptance.

On your mat, carpet, or anywhere you find the need to rest, Childs Pose is there for you. A gentle opening of the hips this posture invokes surrender releasing the lower energies in the root chakra at the base of the spine.

Come to your knees, bringing your sit bones towards your heels as you bring your forehead to the mat. Become small like an embryo—chest towards your thighs. Arms may be extended toward the front of the mat with forearms lifted or resting. You may also bring your arms by your side; palms face up for a more relaxed posture modification. If it is more comfortable for you, turn your head to either side, resting your cheek on your mat. If your head does not reach the ground, use a block to bring the floor to you. Breathe here.

For a deepening of this posture, bring your big toes together, your knees the width of the mat. You will feel your hip flexors open here. Allow your belly to be soft and heavy between your thighs. Let go. Sink into your hips with long, deep inhales and exhales.

Bring awareness into your lower back. Feel the energy stretch across your lower back and hips. Breathe into the tension. Stay here for as long as your body or mind will allow. Childs pose is a posture that will enable you to sink in deeply. Marinate in its depth!

Meditation:

Since we have been able to speak, we have been asking Why of the universe. Why is the sky blue? Why do dogs bark? Why does the fire burn, why, why, why? It is in our nature to question that which we do not understand. Throughout life, we experience pain and suffering. Somewhere in between, we stopped asking why. We stopped fighting for ourselves. We gave up! When we question why we send out an energy of change. We do not settle for what is right before us; we seek the truth. May you always ask why when you are not in alignment with your truth. May those answers provide you with the knowledge to stand on a platform of love for yourself, letting fear fall away. When operating from fear, we choose what is most comfortable. Our old thoughts, feelings, and emotions dictated those choices. But now you know better! Now you have empowered yourself to question why! Self-actualization is you ascending towards a merging with your higher self!

Please sit in a comfortable position on your mat, floor, or cushion for this week's meditation. Your legs may be crossed, and support may be placed under the knees or ankles to add comfort. A block or pillow under the tail bone will add balance and help keep the spine erect.

Let's begin by drawing attention to the natural breath of the body. Do not create an active breath here, taking a few moments to breathe naturally, observing where your breath lands. Notice areas of tension in your body; use your breath to soften you.

When my middle son was five years old, he overheard me yelling at his Brother. He walked into the room I was in, looked at me square in the face, and said, "Mamma, air is the softest thing in the whole world!" I tell that story often when teaching how to use the breath to soften the body. I imagine a billowy cloud leaning into my tight spots encouraging me to unwind.

As you sit, imagine your soft cloud drawing into your body with your breath. Imagine this cloud leaning into your tension. Softening you as you inhale and exhale. Feel the release as you gently let go.

Now bring awareness to the crown of your head. Feel a heaviness over your eyes as, with closed eyes, you gaze upward towards your crown.

Above your head, a golden light illuminates your entire being like a halo of love shining brightly into space. Feel your body in space, begin at the crown of the head, traveling down over the shoulders, arms, hands, chest, belly, hips, legs, and feet. Feel your body hovering in space; notice how space feels around you.

Now bring awareness to your toes, feel the space between your toes, and fill that space with light. Feel the distance between your legs and arms, the area between each finger, the space between your arms and your side body, and space all-around your neck and head, above you and below you.

Now bring your attention to your heart feel the light before it and behind it. From your heart space, see a spinning vortex of energy. Inside this vortex, a key hovers suspended in space. Energy spins around it, but the key is still. Reach into the energy and take hold of the key. Feel the key in your hand, press it against your palm, squeeze it tightly.

Imagine your heart space containing your why. Use the key to unlock you're why and observe it as it projects before you. Information may come in the form of visions, words, memories, or any other shape your higher self chooses to use to speak directly to you. The core of your why lives within the energy of your heart. Observe it and feel what you feel when you see it in front of you. Take in its meaning.

Feel you're why wash over your body as it penetrates every cell, infuses into your breath, and bathes you in its energy. You have all that you need, you have you're why, and it is enough. Sit a few moments here as this energy nurtures you.

In a few moments, come back into your physical space. Slowly open your eyes and reemerge, awakened and empowered.

Gratitude:

This week's practice of gratitude will ask you to seek beyond the surface for appreciation. It is easy to list what is right in front of us. These are the superficial things that make our lives comfortable and allow us to recognize and pay homage to the people around us who help us and bring us joy. These things are good and should be acknowledged.

For the sake of this particular list of gratitude, I encourage you to sink deeper into your mind to extract beyond the surface that which you are grateful. Moments in time that had significant impacts. Small gestures that offered an exchange of love. Hit the rewind button back to your childhood and adolescence to find the things that are still alive in your memories. They have not disappeared, and it is vital to experience finding them and showing gratitude for them. This gratitude practice offers us the positive imprints that never left us and are still vibrating within! Start today with just one from very far back in time. Use description as your journal; each day, find one or two more. Think hard and long. These memories are there waiting for you; they want to see you smile!

Worth!!!!!! Week Five, it's time to rejoice!

Look how far you have come! Open your journal and reread all you have accomplished! You set a goal, showed up for yourself, and did the hard, uncomfortable work to create change in your life! I am so proud of you, and I know because you have adapted a self-love mindset, you are proud of yourself! Congratulations, you are so worthy! You have always been worthy of this feeling; remember it is your birthright to love yourself. No one can take that from you!

Over the last five weeks, you have examined hard emotions. It is not an easy task to dedicate time out of your day towards transformation. You have arrived within yourself. Through this journey, you have experienced opening your body, settling your mind, changing your habits, and reconstructing your thoughts and actions. You, my friend, have done so much! Now it's time to take this newfound energy and apply it to your everyday life. You will notice that as you move through each day up against challenges, your perspective is changed. Perhaps your body no longer has a physical reaction to the events unfolding around you? With continued practice, you will notice even more strength and love for yourself. Creating boundaries will come more comfortable to you. The physical practice of yoga has allowed stuck energy to move out of your body. You have physically and emotionally grown and have gained strength within and without. This alone is a reason to celebrate!

Each meditation that I channeled for you is a gift from the spirit. These meditations put your mind and body through experiences to rewire your channels of thought. With each practice, you went through your mind, fed your body a healing and transformational experience. The neuropathways in your mind fired up and responded! You have adopted new perspectives and have changed the lens through which you were viewing your life. The power of this transformation is significant!

You are probably thinking at this point, "now what?" Yes, you are feeling good, and you have accomplished a goal of completion. But here, the real works begins as you put into practice new habits. Being out in the world faced with adversity, challenges, and change, you will notice your triggers. With this breathe and remember, you have the tools to respond to the world differently, from a place of love and compassion. Feeling self-love is not walking around all day with rose-colored glasses floating on a cloud not affected by your environment. Loving yourself means you understand what is right and healthy for you, knowing you are worthy of saying no, creating boundaries, and practicing compassion for yourself. This energy bleeds into the world around you. You will begin to manifest experiences that support your loving thoughts and actions. The universe will provide you every opportunity to experience what you think and feel. Continue with your practice of yoga, meditation, reflection, and gratitude for what is right and good for you. With the energy you send out into the world, you will notice how life begins to mold around you to support it!

Let's dive into some final questions that will help you identify that things have changed for you!

- **Describe what feeling empowered means to you?**

- **How do you anticipate handling conflict in your future?**

- **When feeling triggered by past programs, how will you create a boundary based on self-love?**

- **Give an example of something or someone that in your past has triggered you emotionally. Explain how your past programs dictated a reaction and how your present awareness will respond.**

Take some time to settle into these newfound realizations. You are a changed person. Continue to observe yourself as you move through each day with challenges and old habits redirecting you back into fear. You have tools now. Your mind is practicing awareness; your body is practicing letting go. I can assure you that you will fall back into your old beliefs. Your belief system has been in place for a very long time. I can also ensure that with continued dedication to self-awareness and love, you will override old habits and create new thoughts to support the positive experiences you manifest! Practice, practice, practice!

A Personal Story:

How I knew I loved myself!

My entire life, I battled self-love. As you have read throughout this book, In my past, I have made choices based on fear from the created programs from a very young age. I experienced my life with ups and downs, sometimes getting close to a definition of happiness but inevitably falling short due to my self-sabotage. It was not until I nearly lost my life that I realized my lack of self-love was the reason why my children almost lost their Mother. As I moved into my future, there was no alternative but to patiently do the hard work of investigating my patterns and behaviors to make the life-lasting change towards positivity. A life filled with love and compassion!

This began by looking at the decisions I had to make in my daily life and observing my habitual reactions. I practiced pausing to ask myself, "am I reacting or responding?" I gave myself space to think about the most compassionate way to make decisions based on loving myself first.

Unfortunately, when we begin to put ourselves first, there is usually an adverse reaction from those closest to us. Our old ways of behaving are predictable and comfortable for the people in our lives. Those around you operating from the ego; will not like your new perspective. It is the sad realization that comes with self-love. Those who can not honor your choices to live compassionately in your body will inevitably fall away. Remember the soul's contract; not everyone stays forever in our lives. Perhaps the people who present the most significant resistance are our most prominent teachers!

Loving myself is a daily practice in listening to my thoughts, acknowledging where they come from, and responding with love. You will discover, with daily routine, less negative fearful thinking, and more future-forward inspiration! A practice in yoga, meditation, reflection, and gratitude brings you closer to your higher self. Connecting to the higher self clears the pathway for ideas and positive inspiration! You will notice that you will feel alive and excited with each day you practice!

After my illness, I quietly set down the burden of a business that defined me for six years of my life. I confidently walked away from an income I depended on into an unknown future. Self-love restored my faith! Since then, I have created opportunities to grow and expand through service to others. I am joyful, fulfilled, and satisfied with my life. Knowing that I am worthy of greatness sends out new signals to my brain to recognize opportunities to express my inner strengths. I live a purpose-filled life; this, too, can be your reality! You can and will have the change you long for if you dedicate parts of your day to loving yourself. Make this practice part of your self-care routine. There is nothing to give when you're well is empty. The practice of yoga, meditation, reflection, and gratitude fills your well with light and love. All you need to manifest positive change is available for you within the practice. Watch as your life magically evolves into more abundance, health, and happiness! Gone are the days of worrying about what other people think. Gone is the self-doubt and anxiety. Gone is the fear! One thing I have repeatedly told my students throughout the years is "it is perfectly acceptable to say no when you do so with compassion." if at that point you are still met with adversity, your eyes are open to truth.

Mission Statement:

I live my life owning that I am worthy of kindness, understanding, compassion, peace, and love. I hold myself to the highest vibration of light and live within the energy of this light. My worth is valuable to me. I am happy, successful, and abundant because I am worthy of all that is right and good in my life!

Asana:

Over the last five weeks, you have practiced poses to reconnect you to self, move energy in your body, and ground you to your intentions. Having done this, you have gained strength, flexibility, and an overall sense of well-being within! Now it is time to put all five postures together. This practice may start out moving slowly. If you are not an active yogi, the asana is probably still uncomfortable and a bit foreign to your mind and body. With a daily devotion to your yoga practice, you will discover ease. In time you will flow in and out of the postures.

Let's begin.

Your yoga sequence is listed below.

1. Sukasana- Easy Seat
2. Pranayama-Breath work
3. Tadasana- Mountain
4. Bidalasana-Cat/Cow
5. Virabhadrasana 1- Warrior 1, with Goddess Arms
6. Balasana- Childs Pose

Meditation:

Dear One, you have emerged from the ashes vibrant and full of life! May the blessings from the spirit continue to ignite your passions and guide your intentions.

For this meditation, take Savasana pose; it will be nurturing to practice this visualization after your yoga practice or anytime you feel weak, fearful, or full of worry. The love within you is the spark that lights the flame of your life. Allow that spark to brighten your path so your truth may continue to reveal itself to you.

Begin by centering with a focus on your breath. Long deep inhale, long deep exhale. Remain like this as you go through a scan of your body. Encourage each part of your body to feel relaxed and heavy. Begin with your feet and work your way to the crown of your head. Breathe in, expand, breathe out, relaxed, and heavy.

At this moment, you have all that you need. Bring your awareness to the emotion of love deep within your heart space. As you inhale, visualize your heart expanding; as you exhale, see your heart contracting into the energy of love. Your heart is love and grows in the strength of love with each breath you take.

Bring now your awareness to the muscles of your face. Soften your face and feel the energy of your third eye chakra, located in between your eyebrows. With your eyes closed, eyelids feeling heavy over your eyes, peer into the third eye. Your third eye is your internal compass revealing to you your true north.

As you continue to follow the flow of your breath, long deep inhale, long deep exhale, take a moment to speak to your heart. Give your heart permission to release any unwanted emotions. Tell your heart, "at this moment; I give permission to release that which does not serve me."

Allow any images to appear to you in the space of your third eye. As you observe what your heart is releasing, do not label or judge the experience. Simply be, watching what is purging from your heart. As you view the images your heart sends to your third eye, acknowledge them for the lessons they have taught you, and gratefully send them into the distant light of the universe.

Continue with this practice until there is no longer an image in your mind. Once you have let it go entirely, sink deeply into your breath as you feel your heart fully expanded in a renewed energy of love and light. Stay in this space for as long as your body will allow. Give thanks for the experience as you feel gratitude fill your heart, mind, and body.

Gratitude:

I hope that having gotten this far, you feel incredibly grateful for so many attributes in your life! The simplest things may feel like an enormous gift today. The practice of gratitude is the gift that continues to give back without fail. The surest way to stay centered on your path of transforming and enlightenment is to be grateful. Please practice gratitude daily. This practice's vibration is far more powerful when taken out of the mind and put into action through journaling or some other form of action. For many years I would send an email to myself with the mailing address "Dear Universe" hitting the send button as I sent my intentions and gratitude felt very exciting and powerful. In practicing gratitude, you will reap the reward of manifesting your dreams. The law of the universe is concrete. There is no other way around it. You reap what you sow. I hope the garden of thought you are planting is fed with gratitude daily.

For this week, let's celebrate your good feelings of self-worth and love! When manifesting our greatest reality, we own the abundance and prosperity we seek through giving thanks for it in our lives. Though it may only be an idea since all things are energy, the idea of your dreams is just a form it has taken until it is fully realized in your life!

You are worthy of everything you have ever desired. Our ideas and inspiration are born from the higher self. The higher self is all-seeing and knowing. The energy of your superconscious mind is constantly funneling new ideas to you. Until now, you may not have realized your thoughts as a message from source. Now in the space of worthiness and love, you know the truth. Whatever positive inspiration you feel comes directly to you from your higher states of consciousness! It is time to give thanks for your open heart and mind and command through gratitude a new reality!

Take some time to think about your goals. Where do you want to be in 6 months from now, a year from now, five years from now? Where do you want to be living, what type of lifestyle do you want? Who are the people in your life in your future? What kinds of relationships fulfill you? Think big here. Remember, your mind is full of the energy of love! Everything you desire is possible with the right energy!

Construct a letter of gratitude that thanks the universe for your life. Be descriptive with your words. You are writing this letter as if all you want is already here. Take a moment to think about your heart's desires; remember they come from your higher self. In doing so, feel the manifestation of your ideas. Feel in your mind, and body the positive emotions that accompany receiving what you want! Your vibrations are magnified in your good feelings.

My friend, you have made it. You took the path less traveled, the high road, and you have made it to the summit! I wrote this book as a means of service. I hope this journey has given you tools to aid you on your path back to yourself, your true self, the self you were born to be. Remember the love you feel will go in and out of your life as you continue to learn and grow. I promise you many more knockdowns, much more pain, and even more sorrow. That is life. What I also promise you, if you commit to your practice and trust the process of self-actualization, a better understanding of yourself and less time in the trenches of self-pity. With practice, there will be more good times than bad times. There will be more joy, more excellent health, more love, and more happiness. Always listen to the voice of the higher self, follow your gut instincts. Your body will always guide you in the right direction. I live by that belief! If something does not feel right, then it's not right! Don't second guess your feelings; they are your guide to less struggle and more peace.

It has been my most incredible privilege and honor to lead you through this journey. I feel incredibly humbled and blessed to be of service to you, and I

hope you will continue with your good intentions for an abundant life! May all that life has to offer to be at your feet. May you know and experience unconditional love from your source. May you have freedom in all that you do, and may your pain be lessened by your perspective. YOU ARE WORTHY! Now, go and throw yourself a party; you have earned a celebration; you are worthy of it!

Namaste,
Shannon

Printed in the United States
By Bookmasters